Starting Again

A Divorce Recovery Program

SANDRA SCOTT

DISCIPLESHIP RESOURCES

P.O. BOX 840 • NASHVILLE, TENNESSEE 37202-0840

www.discipleshipresources.org

Reprinted 1999

Cover and book design by Sharon Anderson

ISBN 0-88177-217-8

Library of Congress Catalog Card No. 97-66503

DR217

Table of Contents

Dedicated to my children, Sean and Stephanie.

Foreward

This began as a six-week, interactive, group program that I developed at the request of my church pastor at Orchard Lake Community Church, Presbyterian. He wanted something to offer those in the congregation who were recovering from the loss of a spouse through divorce or death. I was in graduate school working on a degree in counseling, and I was also in the middle of my own very painful divorce process.

As I looked at what I needed for healing, and as I talked with others going through divorce, I began to realize the similarities of feelings and experiences as well as the great need for a program to facilitate the healing process. The program that resulted helped both me and others through the recovery process.

Over time the program has been refined based on participant's feedback regarding their needs and new issues that emerged, as well as the information I continued to gather from others in my field.

Shortly after I started this program, I became involved in various leadership roles in single adult ministry. That, too, has had a great impact on the writing of this book.

I've tried to include some things I see people struggling with—things they either can't express, or don't feel free to express. I've also tried to address some very practical issues.

Introduction

Divorced. Suddenly single. Suddenly alone. Suddenly life has a tear in it, and a part of your own personal history is ripped from you. It means life will never be the same.

The changes that are then forced upon you are painful, inconvenient, and uncomfortable. Adjustments must be made. Even if it is a positive move, such as separating yourself from abuse, there is still a period of adjustment as you move in a new direction with a new perspective.

The divorce experience is different for each individual. As you read this book or participate in a divorce recovery program, you will need to use the parts that are helpful and relate them to your own life. However, even if some of the material does not relate to your own situation, it may help you to better understand the perspective of others you know.

I too have gone through a divorce. In looking back I recognize two things that no one said to me but that I desperately needed to hear to recover. The two most important things to know at the time of a divorce are

1. The feelings you are experiencing are a necessary and normal response.
2. The pain will not last forever.

It is important that we grieve our losses, grow from them, and then go on. Some losses eventually just work themselves out with a period of transition and then a gradual refilling of life with other things. But with a divorce, there is a forced change of lifestyle. The feelings of failure that often accompany divorce may slow our recovery process.

People around us are often uncomfortable with our pain, and they may try to rush us too quickly toward "getting on with life." Even a recovery program can focus so heavily on a speedy forward look, optimism, and getting back into the swing of activities that we cover up our wounds rather than allowing them to heal. Rushing too quickly through the recovery process increases the chances of repeating former unhelpful behaviors.

Most people who are going through a divorce want to understand what happened to them—not for blaming but for learning. This is appropriate and responsible. Ignorance is never bliss. What we don't know can, and will, hurt us. The constant search for "why" can keep us stuck, but learning to understand is the oil to ease moving forward. It isn't what happens to us but how we handle what happens to us that ultimately matters. And the ability to handle a situation well requires knowledge and understanding.

This book is designed to be used either individually or with a group. It is written from a Christian faith perspective. The program has been conducted in a number of churches of different denominations as well as in secular settings.

SECTION ONE

First Grieve

HELP!

The purpose of a recovery program is to provide a place of support and encouragement, a place where we can each tell our story and be heard, a place where people will understand the pain and problems we are facing as we wade through the process of regaining equilibrium.

A recovery program is a place where we can find unconditional acceptance, where we can hear others' experiences, and where we can share thoughts and feelings. Equally important, it provides an opportunity to be reassured that we are not going crazy, that we are not dying, and that we will not always stay where we are now.

A divorce recovery program also provides new tools and information. It offers new information to help us unravel what is happening to us and a new view of ourselves and our relationships to help us move into the future.

A recovery program can be helpful both for those who did not want a divorce and for those who may have initiated the divorce. Whatever brings us to the starting point of recovery, it is clear that we must move through the pain to leave the pain. A recovery program helps clean old wounds so that healing can begin.

Recovery can begin at different points in people's lives. Some people begin to collect themselves and take steps toward personal mental health before the divorce is final. For others, recovery can only start at the point of separation or the final decree. Some people take a "business as usual" attitude, filling their time with new people, work, or activities, only to discover that they are repeating behaviors that caused them problems in the past. For these people recovery may not begin until long after the divorce is final. For some who refuse to do the recovery "work," life may go on without much growth or real recovery.

A recovery program represents hope—something those going through divorce may not have experienced for a while but desperately need to move forward in life.

LOSSES

The first thing you think of when asked what you lost by being divorced is your spouse. It doesn't take long, however, to realize that there are many other losses that may represent an even greater loss on a daily and long-term basis than the loss of your marriage partner. They are the things that were part of life because that person was in your life, losses that take longer to get over and are usually harder to get beyond than just not having that person around.

Your social life is different when you are part of a couple instead of single. Your plans for the future, for retirement, for travel, and for other activities all change because you are now single. Even if you remarry, your new choices may be limited, compared to the first marriage, because of such things as children or prior financial obligations.

Most people have no way to anticipate the number and depth of losses incurred by divorce. That is why it is such a shock. It is particularly difficult for onlookers to fully comprehend all that is lost or for friends and family to understand and empathize with the upheaval divorced families experience. Because it is difficult to find the support of people who truly understand their situation, divorced people are often overwhelmed with isolation.

On page 17 is a list of typical losses frequently associated with divorce. Before you look at the list, make your own list of the losses you have experienced because of divorce. After you have completed your list, compare it to the list on page 17. How do they compare? Are there things that you want to add to your list?

MY LOSSES

[blank box]

FEELINGS

Now, make a list of the feelings you have experienced as a result of the losses you identified. Remember that there is a difference between thoughts and feelings. Feelings are expressed in words that paint a picture. You get a definite and immediate image of what the word is saying with words such as *warm, cold, frightened, joyful, lonely, lost,* and many others. If someone says, "I feel that...," he or she has actually misspoken. When you use the word *that,* you are expressing something you think, not feel. Look at each loss you have listed and ask yourself, "How does that loss make me feel?"

There is no moral value to feelings; they are not right or wrong—they just are. The right or wrong begins when we respond appropriately or inappropriately to our feelings. After you have listed the feelings you have experienced, compare them to the list on page 18.

Chapter One – Losses and Feelings

MY FEELINGS

EXPRESSING FEELINGS

Feelings of outrage, bitterness, or resentment are extensions of normal grieving for all kinds of losses. With divorce there may be additional bad memories and feelings of pain and injustice that slow the grieving process. The legal action to settle property and custody division can add to the adversarial nature of divorce, prolonging and further complicating the grieving.

When these losses and feelings are shared within a group, you can begin to hear, see, and understand differences in the ways people grieve and the differences in their losses. Interacting with both men and women who have been divorced creates better understanding, softens one's own positions, and diffuses some of one's own anger.

An important part of recovery is for people to be able to tell their story and to feel and express their feelings. Some people are more private than others, but it is important to know that it is normal to have those needs of expression and to know that you can feel free to act on them, if you choose. A good friend or several good friends who will listen are precious jewels in our lives. But it is advisable to not lean excessively on just one person, to protect that friendship from burnout. How much is enough or too much is a personal issue between you and your friends and family.

Sometimes when people who are divorced or in a bad marriage discuss their feelings with each other, it can turn into a prolonged pity party where there is understanding but not much growth or recovery. Discretion is needed—at a time when our ability to discern may be at its lowest—to determine who you can trust not just to be curious or a gossip.

Keeping a journal is another good tool for expressing feelings and for charting recovery and growth. This is a private notebook in which you can write down all your feelings and thoughts—rational or irrational, kind or cruel. It is for your eyes only, and it is a tool for spilling out your inner pain. Keep your journal in a safe place, out of reach of others. Knowing that no one else will be reading your journal gives you the freedom to be completely honest.

Who we are is a measure of our character and personality. What we do is a choice we make about how to solve our problems. We need to take ownership of our lives. We do not want or need someone to fix us or tell us what we should do. We want people who will support us (even when they cannot support our choices or behaviors) so that we can make the best decisions for ourselves. That does not mean that we do not want or need suggestions or information, but the application is our responsibility. It is then a measure of our real intent, our maturity, and our integrity when we make ourselves accountable for our behaviors.

SEEKING COUNSELING

It may be helpful to see a professional counselor for a while. Your pastor may be able to provide counseling or be able to refer you to a counselor. Pastoral counseling centers, community mental health organizations, and social workers in your community may also be able to provide counseling or referrals. In a counseling situation you can express feelings in a healthy way and in a safe place. Also, while counselors are supportive, they are objective and may have valuable insights not available elsewhere. They can help you stay focused in a positive direction and provide reassurance and encouragement. Counseling can be particularly helpful as you deal with questions of "What did I do wrong?" or "What didn't I do?"

A professional counselor can also be helpful when dealing with issues related to physical, emotional, or substance abuse. Unnecessary guilt and self-blame often accompany these issues. A counselor can help discern areas of real responsibility and legitimate guilt and can help you deal with them.

Chapter One – Losses and Feelings

Throughout the Scriptures we see examples of God speaking and something important happening. In Genesis 1 we read that as God spoke the world was created. When the prophets spoke the words of God, they often warned the people or proclaimed the beginning of a cleansing or healing time. Always there was an element of power and the knowledge that something truly big and important was about to start. There is power in the voice, in saying words.

On the human level, the voice is what makes counseling work—the opportunity to speak one's thoughts and feelings. Our thoughts and feelings have tremendous power over us. When they are freely expressed, they lose their power to bind us. If thoughts and feelings are suppressed, they are pushed down inside us where they can fester like a cancer, making us physically ill or stunting our emotional progress. Expressing them creates a space that can then be filled with new things like "love, joy, peace, patience, kindness, generosity, faithfulness, gentleness, and self-control." (Galatians 5:22-23)

Another reason counseling helps is that the counselor is nonjudgmental and offers unconditional positive regard. That does not mean a blanket of approval of the person's choices or behaviors, but acceptance and validation of their personhood as a fellow human being struggling to cope with and make sense of the difficulties of living. It is necessary to value the person, even if the behavior is reprehensible. When we are treated as precious children of God, we can feel free to look honestly at our behaviors. People who feel safe and free from condemnation can begin to grow.

TYPICAL LOSSES
RESULTING FROM DIVORCE

- family unit
- family traditions
- financial security
- sense of history
- lifestyle
- some friends
- identity
- sex
- affection
- a home
- someone to help in:

  child-rearing

  housework

  home maintenance
- pets
- closest friend
- domestic support
- feeling special

- family pictures
- family vacations
- companionship
- sense of future
- couples activities
- in-laws
- a reason to cook
- a reason to work and plan
- a reason to get out of bed
- someone to talk to
- protection
- social life
- children
- decision-making
- someone to come home to
- someone to dream with
- chance to have children
- feeling valued

TYPICAL FEELINGS
RESULTING FROM LOSS

- anger
- hurt
- frustration
- outrage
- jealousy
- out-of-control
- worthlessness
- hopelessness
- no future
- failure
- weary
- anxious
- torn
- immobilized
- lonely
- abandoned
- physical heartache
- bitter
- discouraged
- used
- misunderstood

- sadness
- fear
- confusion
- embarrassment
- shame
- low self-esteem
- depressed
- helpless
- unlovable
- disbelief
- stressed
- loss of trust
- shocked
- betrayed
- alone
- lost
- resentful
- overwhelmed
- guilty
- discarded
- isolated

The

Grief

Process

IMPORTANCE OF TIME

Time is a healing agent. Time alone does not heal, but it provides space within which the healing process can take place. With the passage of time a certain amount of pain will go away; but real healing depends on what you do within that time. If you rush the grief process, true healing is impaired. Eventually you will have to go back and work through issues you left buried.

A very busy business man, in discussing the recent death of his wife, stated to a friend, "I'll be glad when a month has passed." His bewildered friend asked, "Why? What happens in a month?" "Then I'll be over this," was the reply. The man had given himself one month to grieve and recover from the loss of a significant part of his life and his history. The man soon discovered that it isn't that simple. We are not designed to adjust that quickly to loss.

Taking time for grief is an important ingredient in healing. Not just time, but time spent productively, time going through the process, not around it, time spent making adjustments and allowing those adjustments to help you form a new and a different part of your life.

Adjusting to loss and change also takes energy. Grieving drains and exhausts. At times, the natural response is to "cocoon," to hide out for a while in a place of safety. For some people this is expressed through a rigid schedule that allows no time to think or feel. Others stay at home all the time or have an excessive need for sleep. Some people lose themselves in work or other activities like watching television. The ability to function effectively in various areas of life may be impaired for a while.

It is important to be gentle with yourself during this time. Don't be too critical or too demanding of yourself. Remember, when the cocooning has run its course, you will have wings and fly.

EXPLORING THE GRIEVING PROCESS

A number of years ago Elizabeth Kubler Ross did an extensive study on the effect of the death of a loved one. She identified five stages of the grieving process: shock and denial, anger, bargaining, depression, and acceptance.

We now know this grieving process applies to more than just death. Grieving occurs whenever we suffer the loss of something or someone significant to us.

The greater the significance of the loss, the greater the depth of grieving as well as the length of time for recovery. For example, the loss of one's own child is a more significant loss than the loss of a friend's child. The death of a close friend or relative is more painful than the death of a casual acquaintance.

Failure to grieve is not a sign of strength or rugged individualism, but rather an avoidance and denial of feelings. It also prevents healing and growth.

The grief process is a natural, healthy, God-given way to deal with loss. Our culture influences the way we express our grief. In some cultures a stoic response is expected, and in other cultures there may be a period of open weeping and wailing. The important point is that grieving should take place in whatever form is right for the individual.

The following chart highlights the stages of grief and characteristics associated with each stage.

THE GRIEF PROCESS

Grief is a natural, healthy, God-given response to the loss of something or someone of significance to our lives. The degree of significance determines the depth of grieving as well as the length of time.

STAGES	CHARACTERISTICS
1. **Denial**	Denial is nature's way of numbing us temporarily so we will not be scared. Reality is released in manageable pieces at a pace we can handle.
2. **Anger**	The person begins to accept the reality of the situation and frequently responds angrily with "Why me?" Anger may be expressed toward the former spouse, toward others, toward God, and toward self.
3. **Bargaining**	The individual tries to make bargains with God or with others. Questions at this stage include, "What if?" and "If only. . . ."
4. **Depression**	Anger is turned inward. The individual may experience feelings of hopelessness, powerlessness, and deep sadness.
5. **Acceptance**	Life starts to move forward again. The individual • is aware of and able to express feelings. • is able to forgive himself or herself and others. • has a conscious desire and makes a conscious decision to create a new life apart from the person or situation she or he was grieving.

Chapter Two – The Grief Process

FOUR IMPORTANT THINGS TO REMEMBER ABOUT THE GRIEVING PROCESS

- Sadness and memories related to the loss will always remain, but the feelings of anguish and physical pain will diminish as you move through the process.
- The stages of grief generally flow in sequence, but you can bounce back and forth among the stages.
- Grieving is not an option; it is a necessity—either now or later. If delayed, it may become complicated and more intense. It may also be less recognizable later on.
- Grieving is a healing process.

DENIAL

It is comfortable for things to remain the same. We know what to count on. Life has a certain order to it—even if it is not healthy or happy. A loss causes things to never be the same again. Life is different. You are different. Your plans, decisions, and future are all different now. It is painful to accept that. It means you have to change and make changes. It is understandable to want to delay acting on that truth or not accept it at all. We want to make changes in our lives the way we want, not to accommodate what is forced upon us from outside ourselves. It is much more pleasant in the short run to pretend things can remain the same or be modified only as we choose. But, in the long run, that only forestalls and complicates life for us. We may accept the reality intellectually but not emotionally. Denial is a big hurdle to jump.

CHILDREN AND DENIAL

If there are children in the family, they will also go through the stages of grief. It is not uncommon for children to stay in the denial stage much longer than either of their parents. Most children fantasize about their parents getting back together, some for many years. Some children will lie when confronted by other children regarding an impending divorce.

ANGER

Anger is the most unattractive part of grieving. It can be downright ugly at times. During grieving, anger is often expressed inappropriately. Sometimes it is displaced—projected onto something or someone else because you cannot get to who you are really angry at, such as your former spouse. For instance some inappropriate expressions of anger may include

- Yelling, or expressing other forms of frustration at your children or other family members and friends. This is comparable to not being able to talk back to a boss who makes you angry, so you go home and kick the dog.
- Making generalizations about all men or all women. Statements such as "They're all alike," reflect a belief that there is no possibility of a different scenario than the one you have just experienced. These sorts of generalizations indicate that you believe there is nothing you need to explore or learn from the situation.
- Plotting revenge. This can lead you on a very dangerous course that may create even more problems for you. The "good feelings" of getting back at someone are extremely short-lived.
- Taking your anger out on yourself. This may be expressed by
  eating too much
  starting to drink
  using drugs
  considering suicide
  overmedicating
  drinking too much
  spending money lavishly and unnecessarily
  ignoring basic health and hygiene needs
  exhausting yourself by not eating or sleeping properly
  having an affair (especially if your ex-spouse had one)
  driving yourself toward perfection ("I'll show him or her!")
  becoming weak and sickly (the martyr)
- Distancing yourself from your faith community because you are angry with God. It is common to have questions like "Did God cause this to happen?" "Why didn't God prevent this?" "Why did God allow me to get into this situation?" "How can a loving God possibly let things like this happen?"

You have a right to be angry. Anger is a God-given emotion. In the Bible we see God becoming angry over injustice. Anger is not the problem. There is something wrong with a person who cannot feel some anger or outrage. Heaven knows, there are enough injustices in life that deserve it. However, you do not have a right to use anger as an excuse for bad behavior or for hurting others. Destructive ways of expressing anger only create more problems that must eventually be dealt with.

Traditionally, in United States culture, anger is the only emotion men have been given permission to express openly. Therefore, male expressions of anger may conceal feelings of hurt, confusion, frustration, sadness, guilt, embarrassment, and pain, along with real anger. Men have been criticized for their tears. They have been judged weak or not masculine for showing hurt or sadness. Thankfully, this stereotypical image of masculinity is changing, allowing men to become more in touch with the variety of feelings they experience. This increased awareness enhances men's relationships with children, women, and other men.

On the other hand, anger is one emotion women have traditionally been discouraged from expressing. A woman's open expression of anger is likely to make others uncomfortable or even frightened. A woman displaying anger is often described as "hysterical" and "out of control." A woman may cry and express hurt, confusion, frustration, or guilt without the stigma that a display of anger carries.

Some men react to a woman's anger by exhibiting even more anger themselves. They don't know how to handle her anger so they try to squash it. Women's anger is often either ignored by laughing at it or considered a threat. As a society we are so accustomed to viewing women as nurturing, supportive, and stabilizing that we have difficulty reconciling any other view.

For this reason, permission for women to express anger has lagged behind permission for men to express other feelings. The only anger tolerated in a woman is what she shows if her children are in danger, but then only from an obvious, direct predator—certainly not from the subtleties of poverty, abandonment, isolation, abuse, or a myriad of other issues she may be forced to deal with.

It is normal for both parties in a divorce to experience anger. Sometimes the person who did not want the divorce works through her or his anger and moves on with life while the person who initiated the divorce does not move through this stage but stays angry for a long period of time. Often in situations like this the angry person does not have legitimate reason to be angry at his or her spouse and is still attempting to justify the decision to end the marriage.

Then there is the passive/aggressive anger that will not allow a person to leave the marriage, but will cause her or him to push, humiliate, abuse, or not cooperate or contribute anything to the relationship to such an extent that the mate is finally forced to start the divorce action. Passive/aggressive behavior is really aggression disguised as passivity. It is cowardly and avoids taking responsibility for one's choices. Examples of passive/aggressive behavior may include

- shutting someone out financially, giving no access to any of the financial resources.
- selling or destroying the spouse's personal property.
- displaying frustration or anger at someone or something dear to the spouse, such as children, pets, friends, and family.
- abandonment.
- abuse.
- public humiliation, such as flaunting a relationship with another person, public fighting, or demeaning the spouse in front of others.

Constructive means of expressing anger begin with exactly that—expressing it. You need to talk about your hurt feelings—the pain, the bitterness, the resentment, and the many other feelings that are part of the grieving process. Probably the best place to do that is out loud, privately, with yourself and God. God's unconditional love is available to you in the midst of your darkest feelings. There is nothing you can say to God that places you beyond the love of God.

Sometimes it helps to beat a pillow, take a walk, run, stomp your feet, scream, and so forth. Do the things that work for you. Sometimes you just need to talk to another person. That is when you should seek a trusted confidant, your pastor, or a professional counselor.

Sometimes when we hear others expressing their anger, we may think we need to provide answers for them. Unless they directly ask for advice, all they really want is to be heard, to have their feelings validated, and to be understood. It is not necessary to agree with what they think or how they are feeling. Just allow them to own and express their feelings (unless it leads to hurtful behavior). At times it may be necessary, as a friend, to try to keep them from doing destructive things. Be gentle and cautious. Dealing with the angry feelings is a significant part of the grieving process. The way that others respond to the anger can influence the person's willingness to deal with these feelings.

Constructive anger seeks real solutions, not fantasy. It looks for healthy ways to resolve itself. Ultimately, you have to allow yourself to feel your feelings—however irrational they may be for now—and find healthy and responsible ways to express those feelings.

CHILDREN AND ANGER

Children need to be encouraged to discuss their feelings—all their feelings, including anger. They also need to be given opportunities to express their feelings in appropriate ways. If a child is denied such opportunities or is punished for showing anger, the child may withdraw or act out the anger in socially inappropriate ways. Inappropriate anger may be directed toward siblings, pets, classmates, or other significant adults in the child's life.

Children will often express anger and display hostility toward the parent who showed the most responsibility toward them. That is because the children feel safer to express their anger with that parent. They may be unconsciously afraid that if they express it to the parent they are more angry with, they will lose what little contact they have left with that parent. This fear is a heavy price for children. It does great damage.

Adults are often frightened or intimidated by their children's anger. Parents may feel their children are out of control. At a time when the parents may be feeling overwhelmed by their own feelings, it can be difficult to deal with the children's feelings. Because children usually want to please their parents and because they know they are dependent upon their parents, children may inadvertently receive the message that they should submerge their own feelings to protect their parents from any more "bad news."

Many families find it helpful for their children to participate in a divorce recovery program designed specifically for children. These programs provide additional opportunities for children to express their feelings in a safe environment.

BARGAINING

The bargaining stage is interesting. It is when you try to play games with yourself, God, or the missing spouse. You are seeking to minimize your pain and the reality of the situation.

Bargaining may or may not include the other party. Bargaining is different from negotiating conflict or differences to restore or preserve a relationship. Negotiation requires two people. Then it becomes problem solving. (Marriage counseling is problem solving with the help of a facilitator.)

Bargaining is similar to the denial stage in that there is an unreality to it. The denial stage pretends it didn't happen. Bargaining acknowledges that it happened, but it looks for imaginary ways to "fix it" or to turn back the clock and prevent it. Bargaining scenarios may sound something like these.

If only I had been thinner, had a college degree, had been prettier, had been a better house-keeper, or had not been afraid to ski, he would not have cheated on me.

Perhaps. Or he still may have cheated. That is a question of his character. He had a responsibility to discuss with you the things that bothered him and the things he would have liked you to do differently. You both had a responsibility to discuss the issues and attempt to negotiate a resolution. However, there are some things over which you have no control, such as the face you were born with. Continuing to rehash things about yourself that are beyond your control keeps you stuck and running in circles instead of moving forward.

What if I lose weight, get a face lift, go back to college, and take up skiing?

Who is to say what would happen. Again, if it is something over which you have some control and you are willing to change or negotiate, perhaps it could make a difference. However, by the time someone has left a relationship, the interest and commitment to discussion are usually non-existent. Chances are those are not the real reasons the person left the relationship anyway. They are usually the surface excuses. The real, underlying reasons are often things such as:

- involvement with someone else
- a midlife crisis
- substance abuse
- dissatisfaction with self
- lack of communication
- a need to always be in control
- fear of aging and dying

What if I give up playing softball three times a week, learn to dance, and promise not to watch Monday night football?

That may have done some good before the divorce or separation, but the chances are good that she is tired of nagging to get time and attention from you. Or she may have diverted her attention to building her own life—going back to school, getting a job she enjoys, focusing on herself instead of only on you and the family. She may be learning country/western line dances that do not even require a partner, so she doesn't care now whether or not you learn to dance.

As you move through this stage, it is helpful to evaluate your own part in the demise of the relationship; but it is equally important to be realistic about your partner's part. Many times one or the other spouse has just never grown up. He or she may be self-centered and spoiled. Some people have never made the necessary break from their family of origin to become their own person and bond with a spouse. Some may be so personally insecure or low in self-esteem that they are caught up in one or many diversions or obsessions that prevent a stable marriage or family life. Substance abuse, extramarital affairs, refusal to work, doing nothing but work, jealousy, suspicion, various addictions (shopping, gambling, constant activities, and any number of others) can so disrupt a relationship that for security or sanity it becomes necessary for one of the partners to initiate a divorce, regardless of their own desire to work things out.

Part of the recovery and growth process is an honest examination of one's own contribution to the problems. However, a martyr's acceptance of blame that is not real is a sign of an unhealthy lack of knowledge or information, not a magnanimous gesture or sign of humility.

We can deceive ourselves indefinitely, if we choose, but that will not move us forward. We can deny the situation, refuse to work through to acceptance, or refuse to look at our own lives to avoid repeating things that need to be changed. Neither will it be of any value to heap unnecessary or undeserved coals onto ourselves. We need to make a searching and fearless moral inventory of ourselves.

BARGAINING AND CHILDREN

Children frequently believe that they are somehow responsible for the divorce. They think that if they had been "good," mom and dad would not have gotten a divorce. A child may make secret promises to God that if the parents reconcile he or she will never be "bad" again. The fantasy that the parents will reunite dies very slowly, and the child may try to bargain with both God and his or her parents to create a reconciliation. Children may "act out" with illness or bad behavior hoping to reunite the parents.

DEPRESSION

Depression has been described as anger turned inward. It is anger that comes from deep sadness accompanied by a sense of helplessness. It is often characterized by a feeling of hopelessness. I remember thinking, "What will become of me?" "I have no future." "How can I survive this?"

Symptoms of depression include

- a persistent sad, anxious, or "empty" mood
- feelings of hopelessness and pessimism

- feelings of guilt, worthlessness, and helplessness
- loss of interest or pleasure in hobbies and activities that you once enjoyed
- loss of interest in sex
- insomnia, early-morning awakening, or oversleeping
- appetite and/or weight loss or overeating and weight gain
- decreased energy, fatigue, being "slowed down"
- thoughts of death or suicide, suicide attempts
- restlessness, irritability
- difficulty concentrating, remembering, making decisions
- persistent physical symptoms that do not respond to treatment, such as headaches, digestive orders, and chronic pain

All of these symptoms need not be present for depression to exist. During the grieving process, depression is a normal phase; however, depression that goes too long or too deep needs to be addressed as a separate issue. How long is too long is a tough judgment, since each person is unique. What is normal for one person may be dangerous to another. It is important to take the time and effort to really know ourselves and to have feedback from trusted friends or a professional counselor.

Depression is more likely to occur in women. This may be due to the traditional intolerance of women expressing anger. At the same time, women are more likely to recognize and acknowledge their depression and to seek help.

Some men think of depression as unmanly or a weakness. Those men may simply turn to diversions to fill the void of their loss. Others may contemplate or commit suicide.

Depression is greatly influenced by the level of expectations we have. In cultures where there are few expectations of life there is minimal depression. Religious faith and strong family and community support are important assets that can help a person successfully handle depression.

Depression resulting from anger with people or situations over which you have no control (including God) can be prolonged. If the depression is a result of anger that is focused on yourself, you can have some control over it. As you begin to sort out what is real, legitimate responsibility and what is assumed responsibility—the part of life that just "is" or "happens"—you can begin to constructively work your way out of depression. As you begin to look within, you begin to be able to objectify the anger, making it easier to do something about it and get rid of it.

A lack of hope or unrealistic expectations of life can also prolong depression. They only reinforce the feeling that there is not much to look forward to or get excited about.

Your willingness to be actively involved in your own recovery will directly determine the quality of the rest of your life. It determines whether you will cross the line from depression to acceptance, becoming better instead of bitter. The choice is yours—one you must make again and again. Recovery is an ongoing process, not a one-time "quick fix."

CHILDREN AND DEPRESSION

As a child's belief that the parents will reunite begins to fade, the child may go through a time of depression. As it is in the anger stage, it is important for children to be able to express their feelings in a safe environment. Children need to be reassured that although the parents are no longer husband and wife, they are still mother and father to the children.

Special Issues

Each divorce has unique dynamics that have an impact upon the recovery process. In this chapter we will examine a variety of issues that may be involved in divorces. As you read, identify those issues that apply to your situation.

ABUSE

In most situations professional counselors and helping friends are best advised to take a noncon-frontational approach. The exception to this is when abuse is occurring. Then there is a need to immediately insist on accountability. There is an obligation to offer aid and/or sanctuary to the victims. It is appropriate to help the victims out of harm's way. This is especially true if there is physical abuse. However, verbal, psychological, or emotional abuse is just as devastating and damaging, although it may not be as obvious. It should be identified to the victim as what it is—abuse.

Victims don't always see that they are being abused. They are accustomed to making excuses for the perpetrator to justify in their own minds the fact that they stay in the relationship. They may be more frightened of change than confident of their ability to make the necessary changes. Or their lives have become comfortably familiar, even while they are being abused. Change takes courage, so it is not always easy to leave an abusive relationship. It may seem obvious to outsiders; but when you are living in an abusive situation day after day, concentrating on survival, it is very hard to see clearly what is actually going on or the extent of the problem. It is even harder to see a way out of the danger.

Every person has the right not to be physically, verbally, or emotionally abused. Parents have an obligation and responsibility to protect their children from abuse of any kind. Adult victims who do not recognize themselves as victims may also have difficulty protecting others from abuse.

Whenever you ride an airplane, there is a brief safety check at the beginning of the flight. You are cautioned that if oxygen is needed, you are to put the oxygen mask on yourself first and then on the children around you. You cannot take care of anyone else if you are not taking care of yourself first. You not only have the right to care for yourself but also the responsibility. Self-care is not being selfish or self-centered.

The parent who has not been able to grow and develop in a healthy way is greatly impeded from nurturing a child's healthy developmental process. That child will be fortunate if there is someone else, such as a teacher, friend, or relative, who will act as a role model and protector. It is well documented that people who were abused as children are at increased risk of becoming abusers themselves. It is also common for an adult who had abusive parents to gravitate toward abusive relationships.

There are victims who have been told that harmful behaviors are not abuse but merely appropriate acts to encourage biblical submission. This argument is most often used against women. Great guilt can come to a woman from this message, often immobilizing her. It is bad enough to know that she is a disappointment to her husband, but it is even worse to believe she has failed God.

Years—even centuries—of the misuse of a few passages of Scripture have had a devastating effect on the attitudes of some women about themselves and of men about women. Particularly some of the Pauline passages, such as Ephesians 5:22, have been used out of context. Their selective use has done great harm to relationships between men and women. Sometimes women have been told that "the Bible says you must let your husband do whatever he wants to you." However, if we carefully read the Scriptures we receive a very different message.

The basic message of the gospel is that we are to love God and love one another. Ephesians 5:21-33 compares the marriage relationship to Christ's self-giving relationship to the church. Husbands are admonished to love their wives in the same way they love themselves, nourishing and tenderly caring for the marriage relationship. Wives are told that, likewise, they should respect their husbands. The writer of Ephesians is addressing both husbands and wives when he says, "Be subject to one another out of reverence for Christ." (Ephesians 5:21) These verses clearly imply that marriage is a mutual relationship in which each person is to act with love and respect toward the other. Neither physical nor emotional abuse are consistent with Christian love. There is never scriptural justification for anyone to abuse another person.

You have the right not to be abused. It is not acceptable to abuse another. Many divorces result from some type of abuse. Victims often start out blaming themselves—"What did I do wrong?" or "What didn't I do that I should have?"

Most who abuse feel justified in what they are doing at the moment they are doing it. They also do not see their behavior as abusive. They believe the victim is the cause and is, therefore, responsible for the treatment he or she receives. Abusers of this type not only need to be educated about abuse but need to be restrained from continuing the abuse.

In many abusive situations the abusing spouse expresses remorse afterward, promises never to abuse again, and then repeats the abusive pattern. This cycle can usually only be stopped if the abused removes himself or herself from the cycle.

There are other people who genuinely think of themselves as rational, caring human beings, but who may be exhibiting abusive behavior without realizing it. This is particularly true of verbal and emotional abuse. Those individuals will likely respond positively to being made aware of the effect of their abuse. They may feel embarrassed at what they learn, but they are the ones who will want to correct whatever is abusive. The change of behavior in a positive way often greatly improves their communication with others and enhances their relationships.

Some abuse is obvious. When you've been hit, bruised, or beaten up, you know, and everyone else can see, that you have been abused. Other forms of abuse are not as obvious. They include

- verbal assaults
- abandonment
- neglect
- spousal rape
- isolation
- minimizing another's pain
- blaming for imagined offenses
- withholding money and other resources

All are insidious attempts at coercion, threat, and intimidation. The perpetrator "brainwashes" the victim into believing the abuse is deserved while maintaining a position of entitlement for his or her actions.

There is only one answer to abuse: It must be stopped and perpetrators must be held accountable. In cases where the abuser refuses to be accountable and to stop the abusive behavior, the victim must be separated from the abuser. This may involve the need for legal enforcement to ensure the victim is protected. It is extremely important that perpetrators be removed from a situation where they are harming their victims. Abusers must be confronted and stopped, or they will simply find another victim.

Without the support of others (including law enforcement), the victim may feel that his or her only option is to run away. This does not solve the problem. It completely disrupts the life of the victim while leaving the abuser free to continue the abusive pattern with someone else.

Abuse is a choice. The abuser makes a decision to hurt another person. Not alcohol, stress, fear, nor anything else is an acceptable excuse for abuse.

The subtle forms of abuse—the ones that shed no blood or leave no bruises—are harder to detect, but they leave a mark on the soul that heals much more slowly than marks on the body. These nonphysical marks may never heal if they are not recognized. It is very possible to not even know you were abused in a relationship until long after it has ended. Abused individuals who do not understand that they were abused may not recognize the right they have to feel outraged and to protect themselves. They may also be accepting false blame for the situation. Being able to place the blame where it correctly lies is an important element in getting help and stopping the abuse.

Blaming is generally discouraged in our society. However, it is appropriate to recognize responsibility. The abuser may interpret that as blaming. In the absence of understanding the truth of who is responsible, people can be misled into accepting responsibility that is not truly theirs. Responses such as, "You made me angry"; "If you hadn't done that, I wouldn't have reacted that way"; and "I told you not to do that—it's your fault" can paralyze the victim and allow the abuser to feel vindicated.

Why do you need to learn about abuse, especially if you are now out of an abusive relationship? If you were abused and didn't know it or learn from it, you will be open prey for another abusive relationship. Or you may be so affected by that experience that you will not recognize or allow yourself to enter into healthy relationships.

POWER AND CONTROL
VERSES EQUALITY

The "Power and Control Wheel" on page 36 and the "Equality Wheel" on page 38 illustrate two different types of relationships. Use the space below to list characteristics of your own relationships. As you examine the wheels look for similarities between things you have listed and items listed in the wheels. **Note that these wheels were developed by a domestic abuse intervention project that deals specifically with women who are in abusive relationships. Therefore, male pronouns are used to refer to the abuser and female pronouns to the abused. As you use these wheels, you may need to change the pronouns to fit your own situation.**

_____

_____

_____

_____

_____

_____

_____

_____

POWER AND CONTROL WHEEL

1. Using Coercion and Threats
- Threats are statements that promise negative consequences for certain behaviors or actions. For example, "I'll kill you if you ever leave me."
- Coercion is statements or actions that imply, indirectly, negative or positive consequences for certain behaviors or actions. For example, cleaning the house and buying her flowers the day after abuse.

2. Using Intimidation
- Making her afraid by using looks, actions, gestures, intoxication, "silent treatment"
- Smashing things
- Destroying property
- Harming pets
- Displaying weapons
- Yelling
- Stalking
- Slamming doors
- Driving recklessly
- Acting "crazy," invincible, or like "I have nothing to lose"

3. Using Emotional Abuse
- Putting her down
- Making her feel bad about herself
- Calling her names
- Making her think she's crazy
- Playing mind games
- Humiliating her
- Making her feel guilty
- Using things that matter to her against her
- Negatively comparing her to others
- Unreasonable demands or expectations
- "Honeymooning" her
- Perfectionism

4. Using Isolation
- Controlling her access to resources such as birth control, reproductive choices, medical attention, money, education, employment opportunities, family, friends, transportation, phone use
- Using jealousy to justify actions
- Embarrassing her in front of others
- Kidnapping her
- Convincing her that seeing her family or friends is "harmful to our relationship"

5. Using Confusion
- Denying or minimizing the existence, severity, or impact of abusive behavior
- Blaming or otherwise shifting responsibility for abusive behavior
- Lying about, concealing, withholding or omitting information, situations, or behavior to gain advantage
- Pretending to be a victim to gain sympathy, support, or allies
- Using intoxication as an excuse

6. Using Others
- Using the children to relay messages
- Using visitation to harass her
- Threatening to take the children away
- Using custody of the children as leverage
- Abusing the children
- Sexual abuse of the children
- Kidnapping the children
- Degrading her about her relationships
- Using her job, family, friends, religion, etc. as leverage

7. Using Male Privilege (or the Power of Position)
- Defining what men's and women's roles are
- Defining what is and isn't "important"
- Controlling the decision-making process
- Making and enforcing self-serving rules
- Treating her as an inferior
- Acting like the "master of the castle"
- Believing "it's my right to behave this way"
- Acting like God

8. Using Economic Abuse
- Concealing or denying information about finances
- Using family assets without her knowledge or permission
- Preventing her from getting, keeping, or leaving a job
- Damaging her credit rating
- Making her ask for money
- Destroying checkbooks, credit cards, money, or property
- Giving her an allowance

Used by permission of the Domestic Abuse Intervention Project, Duluth, MN.

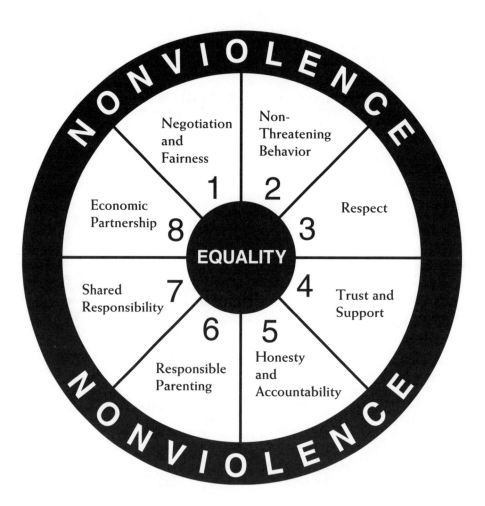

EQUALITY WHEEL

1. Negotiation and Fairness
- Seeking mutually satisfying resolutions to conflict
- Accepting change
- Being willing to compromise

2. Nonthreatening Behavior
- Talking and acting so that she feels safe and comfortable expressing herself and doing things

3. Respect
- Listening nonjudgmentally
- Being emotionally affirming and understanding
- Valuing opinions

4. Trust and Support
- Supporting her goals in life
- Respecting her right to her own feelings, friends, activities, and opinions

5. Honesty and Accountability
- Accepting responsibility for self
- Acknowledging past use of violence
- Admitting being wrong
- Communicating openly and truthfully

6. Responsible Parenting
- Sharing parental responsibilities
- Being a positive nonviolent role model for the children

7. Shared Responsibility
- Mutually agreeing on a fair distribution of work
- Making family decisions together

8. Economic Partnership
- Making money decisions together
- Making sure both partners benefit from financial arrangements

Used by permission of the Domestic Abuse Intervention Project, Duluth, MN.

INFIDELITY

Marriage is a covenant relationship made between a man and a woman. In a service of Christian marriage the couple makes vows before each other, the faith community, and God that they will honor, love, and cherish one another. They also declare that they will be faithful to each other.

Great harm comes to a relationship in which this covenant is broken through infidelity. Infidelity does not always take the form of an extramarital sexual affair. It can also be an emotional betrayal. Like nonphysical abuse, emotional betrayal can be even more insidious than the obvious act of a sexual affair. Infidelity gives the message that something or someone has replaced you in a union that had made you and your spouse a couple.

Repeated infidelity is like repeated blows to an open injury. The first blow creates the open wound while each succeeding blow deepens and widens the already excruciatingly painful injury. Over time, the relationship withers and dies.

The possibility of sexually transmitted diseases multiplies the dangers of extramarital sexual encounters. Pretending to ignore that a sexual affair is occurring is foolhardy. The possibility of getting a sexually transmitted disease adds to the sense of violation, knowing that an unfaithful partner could put you in jeopardy of suffering an illness or even death as a consequence of his or her breach of the relationship.

This is not to say that infidelity has to end a marriage. More often than not, however, it creates a wedge between the partners that is extremely difficult to remove.

CHILDREN

The presence of children in a family where divorce has occurred adds enormous complexity to the recovery process.

The custodial parent experiences the increased responsibility of caring for all of the day-to-day needs of the children. The noncustodial parent feels the loss of time and interaction with the children. Those feelings are understandable and appropriate.

It is very important that the children be reassured that their parents have not ceased to be their parents, even though they are no longer husband and wife. Although it may present significant challenges, it is best if both parents continue to be involved in their children's lives.

If the noncustodial parent has been physically or emotionally absent to the children, the separate homes sometimes facilitate new or expanded quality and quantity time between that parent and child. However, if the inattentiveness or noninvolvement continues, the children may feel even more alienated by the separation. Visits to the noncustodial parent then become times away from more stable support systems, friends, familiar surroundings, and more attentive family members.

It can be difficult for the noncustodial parent to remain significantly involved in his or her children's lives. However, if the parent distances him or herself from the children, or simply disappears, the effect on the children can last a lifetime. The effect on that parent also lasts a lifetime, whether or not he or she ever realizes or acknowledges it.

The issues that most often surface for the custodial parent are financial needs and emotional and physical exhaustion related to trying to meet work, home, and children's needs. For the noncustodial parent, the primary issues are access to the children and the loneliness without them. If either parent moves out of the area, that can cause great anxiety and the pain of longer absences for both the noncustodial parent and the children, as well as added expense for travel and phone calls.

Although the number of men who are custodial parents has risen, the overwhelming majority of custodial parents are women. Because most women still make less money than men, the financial strain is usually greater for her.

The statistics on the financial well-being of divorced women and men are shocking. While there are, of course, many exceptions, generally within three to five years after a divorce, a man's standard of living increases while a woman's decreases. Initially, the man's lifestyle may plunge, but he has greater ability to recover because he is usually making more money and has fewer housing and daily children-related expenses. Studies indicate that nearly half of all divorced fathers pay child support for only a short time or not at all.

Children are the most victimized by divorce. They are innocent bystanders who suffer the greatest losses. We may think that because they remain silent, they are not hurting. But as mentioned in Chapter 2, children also go through the grieving process. Children often think they are to blame for problems between their parents, so they hide their shame. They may hide it in silence or act out behaviors of arrogance, sarcasm, or bullying—all to cover the shame they feel.

Children may be thinking things like: "Maybe I am bad, so I make mom and daddy angry or unhappy. Maybe they don't love me any more, otherwise why would they leave? Why are they angry all the time? I must be doing bad things. If I were better behaved (or smarter, or prettier, or more helpful), they probably wouldn't go away."

The child who acts out with negative behaviors—fighting with siblings or playmates, neglecting school work or chores—may actually be dealing with the divorce better than the child who does not exhibit any angry behavior. Through the negative behavior the child is in effect, saying, "I'm mad. I'm scared. Something's going on that I don't understand and can't control, and I want someone who is bigger and stronger than I to make it right again." However, if the issues they are dealing with are not resolved, it could set them on a dangerous course that may get worse with time.

If children who are acting out their anger are never helped to understand the source of their anger, they make not only their own lives but the lives of others miserable, especially those in whom they have a significant emotional investment.

In the 1970s Judith Wallerstein began the first major study of the long-term effects of divorce on children. The results of the research were reported in the book *Second Chances* (Wallerstien and Blakeslee [Tichnor & Fields, 1989]). In her research and interviews with children and adult children of divorce, she found that the trauma of divorce stays with a child to some extent throughout life. Not only must children deal with the day-to-day effects of divorce, such as change of lifestyle, feeling the void of a missing family member, and so forth; but many children have difficulties in other relationships. Their sense of security, identity, and self-esteem is often impaired. Wallerstein's research indicated that children of divorce are at risk for depression, poor grades, and substance abuse. Many children lost their role models for such virtues as compassion, empathy, patience, courage, loyalty, persistence, positive attitude, creative problem-solving, diplomacy, forgiveness, love, and kindness.

Children of divorce often perceive a message from their parents that "my wants and needs are more important than you." They may believe that they are important to their parents only as long as they don't interfere with what the parents want. Since children tend to see their parents as one unit rather than as two individuals, it is difficult for them to separate the actions and beliefs of their two parents. Even in cases where one person made the decision to leave the marriage, the children may feel abandoned by both parents. This leaves the children believing there is no one whom they can trust or who will look out for them.

TALKING ABOUT THE DIVORCE

Knowing the truth related to the divorce does not mean the child cannot or should not be encouraged to love both parents. Love does not demand perfection. Truth sets us free to love knowingly, in spite of problems. Truth can help children to see their parents as individuals, freeing them from the feeling that they have no one to trust.

In the absence of truth, the imagination fills in the blanks. For a child, imagination unchecked can be a dangerous thing, usually more frightening than the truth. Children need to be reassured that they are not the cause of the divorce. Although they may not verbalize it, children often mistakenly believe that the divorce is their fault.

Children old enough to understand about separation and divorce should be told, in general terms, what has happened and why. Otherwise, they receive the message that marriage is only until you change your mind, divorce is no big deal, or that commitment and vows do not mean anything. A cavalier attitude minimizes the significance of their sadness and their perceptions. It can cause them to suppress their feelings.

Children do not need all the details, and they should never be used as a parent's confidant, counselor, or messenger. Find out what they do know and what they think is happening. Do not lie to them or tell them unnecessary information that they cannot handle. Be gentle and listen. Speak simply with kindness, avoiding sarcasm. Acknowledge the child's loss and the feelings that accompany the loss.

You could say, "Yes, daddy has a problem with alcohol that he is not able to control. It has become dangerous for us to stay together. That makes us all very sad. But that does not mean we don't still care about him and love him. It's all right for you to feel sad. I do too. It's okay to cry."

Or, "Yes, mommy has decided that she does not want to be married to me any longer. She wants to live a different life. But she is divorcing me, not you children. We will both still be part of your lives. We will try to keep things as normal and happy for you as possible. I know this makes you very sad. It's okay to feel sad or angry or hurt. It's okay to talk about your feelings."

Even with the best possible explanations, appropriately designed to fit their level of age and understanding, children will still experience confusion. A child's interpretation is that "something" is more important to the parent than they are. Children instinctively know that they depend totally on their parents for safety, security, and guidance. They can't even imagine a day when they will be able to fully operate on their own.

Therefore, when parents decide to divorce, children automatically become fearful. "Divorce" is a wedge that is now between them and their parents. They may not verbalize it, but the immediate and long-range response is insecurity. The child thinks, "How can this be? She loves me, but she wants to leave me?" "He loves me, but he can walk away from me?"

CHILDREN AND ABUSE

The presence of abuse in the household conveys very negative messages to the children. It will diminish their sense of worth and will lessen their value of others. It will have an impact on their own ability to be good parents one day.

Abusive relationships raise questions like these:

- Is someone always more valuable or more important than the other?
- What is a relationship between two people supposed to be like?
- What does a healthy marriage look like?
- What are the characteristics of a man? of a woman?
- How are people who love each other supposed to behave?
- Does yelling or hitting show love?
- Do I have to be less important than you for you to feel good about yourself?

If we allow abusive or irresponsible behaviors to be modeled to our children, we set them up to be victims or abusers. It takes a great deal of intervention and a lot of re-education to turn that around. Things learned in childhood from our primary caregivers become set in cement. To change them means chipping away for a long time to find the truth.

How many times have you heard, "It would have been better if my parents had divorced." They are often referring to abusive words or actions that went on in front of them. People who make those observations are usually the ones who recognize problems and will probably take care to do things differently. The ones who cannot see issues needing to be addressed are the ones likely to repeat those attitudes and behaviors in their own lives, continuing the cycle.

In cases where abuse exists, the child may not recognize that as a problem—he is used to it, it is all he knows. That puts an additional burden onto the parent who finally chooses to end a marriage. To children, it is the nonabusive parent who is causing them the pain of divorce. The child may carry anger and bitterness against that parent for years or forever, unless they learn the dynamics of abuse. It is a hard decision for a parent to risk that to save the child. It is a sacrificial act. There are some situations in which an abusive parent must be supervised in his or her visitation or denied access for the safety and well-being of the child.

AFTER THE DIVORCE

It is not unusual for children to take their anger and frustration out on the parent they feel safest with, the one they know will never leave them or reject them, the one who will always love and support them no matter what.

When a father leaves the family, he has, in effect, put all the male responsibilities of the household onto his children, especially the son(s). People used to tell a little boy, "You are the man of the house now." Society recognizes the danger of laying that kind of responsibility onto a child and most of us have stopped saying it.

However, even if it is not verbalized by others, boys will feel the added responsibility. Some boys respond to this pressure by assuming premature adult responsibilities. Others respond by rejecting normal and expected household responsibilities.

If it is the mother who leaves, the same scenario is true for daughters.

If something happens to the custodial parent, such as an illness or accident, who is there to fill the void? In trying to rise to the occasion, children can be robbed of a portion of their own childhood. They are thrust into adult roles before they are prepared to handle them. If they see the need, but also see that they are incapable of filling that need, they suffer feelings of guilt, fear, and inadequacy. They may even resist the normal developmental tasks they should be dealing with.

When divorced parents enter into new relationships, they need to remember that their children do not necessarily share their enthusiasm for this new third party. Use discretion in introducing a new "boyfriend" or "girlfriend" to your children.

Life deals some pretty heavy blows at times. Part of the growing experience is learning to navigate the waters of unwanted change. It is important to be a good captain of your ship and have good navigation tools to successfully steer toward the safe port of healthy adulthood.

There are support groups and programs available for children of divorce through schools, churches, and other community programs. Children may find it easier to be open about their feelings in such a program, where they don't have to worry about further upsetting their parents. What is not dealt with is carried and later dumped—usually onto someone else.

In addition to support groups many children find individual counseling helpful as they deal with feelings and issues related to divorce.

HOLIDAYS AND VISITATION

No matter how amicable two people try to be in a divorce, it will still mean a lot of traveling for the children. The children will always feel torn between their love for the noncustodial parent and wanting to be with him or her, and their need for the sense of security that is satisfied by their own room in their own house with their own friends nearby.

There are periods in a child's growing up when their peer relationships are more important to them than family. The moving back and forth between parents that often accompanies divorce interrupts their ability to see and be with their friends. They are constantly starting and stopping their lives. The older they get, the harder it is to leave one home and go to another. They barely settle in and adjust to the transition before it's time to switch back again. There will be birthday parties, sleepovers, little league games, football games, dances—all the activities with their friends, versus going every other weekend to visit their "other home."

For the custodial parent, visitation with the other parent is often a relief, a time he or she can relax from the daily responsibilities of caring for all the needs of the children. For the noncustodial parent, it may offer a chance to reconnect with the children and to try to get back in touch with normal family life.

Both parents may feel guilty. Both know it is the children who are the most inconvenienced and least happy with the arrangement. The children often feel embarrassed about their split lives. At the same time, it is vital that they have two parents. To have them both, the child's life must be split. It is often a difficult situation; however, in most cases it is still better for the children to have both parents in their lives.

It is hard for parents to realize how deeply they offend their children when they do not cooperate regarding visitation or sharing of holidays. If they fight, it adds salt to the already raw wound. It is difficult, however, if one parent refuses to work fairly with the other. Sometimes, no matter how hard one parent tries, the other may be intent on demonstrating power in the situation or may still be battling the divorce itself and thus make every occasion a conflict.

Again, if there are issues of abuse or inappropriate behavior, there can be no consideration of visitation fairness. At that point, the child's safety and welfare are paramount. In those situations, the nonabusing parent may have to make some tough decisions for the welfare of the child. Children do not always understand what is going on and may react in anger to the nonabusing parent.

It is often helpful to get a professional third party to mediate an equitable visitation schedule. A skilled divorce mediator, who is an advocate for the children, can help both parents come to decisions on a variety of issues related to the children. When both parents participate in creating an agreement, both are more likely to honor it than they are when handed an edict from the court. This agreement is not about compromise. With compromise, usually someone feels that they have had to give up something that is important. But if there is good negotiation taking place, with exploration of many options, there can often be a win-win resolution—one where all parties feel that their concerns have been dealt with.

As children grow up, there will be graduations, confirmations, weddings, and other occasions that require cooperation and the setting aside of personal feelings for the sake of the children. Parents should strive to make these happy occasions rather than opportunities to revive old conflicts. Some situations are indeed more difficult to deal with than others. Birthdays, graduation parties, or other celebrations may need to be done with each side of the family. A wedding may stretch everyone to their limits if there are lingering animosities. However, it's not the kind of thing you can do twice—once with each parent and their friends—so some negotiation of ground rules for everyone is necessary.

IN-LAWS AND EXTENDED FAMILY

Sometimes, losing ones in-laws is not a great loss. Most of the time, though, separation of extended family represents losses that cannot be anticipated at the time of a divorce. Grandparents, aunts, uncles, cousins, and all the family members suffer when children are stretched between two households. Sometimes they lose contact with the children altogether. The children then grow up without the benefit of all those people to love, love them, and teach them about life and family.

The family of the spouse who either arbitrarily chooses or causes the divorce is most torn. They face the realization that their son or daughter has made a decision that is hurtful to everyone. They are torn between loyalty to their child and their own pain of seeing the family torn apart. Because the extended family disapproves of the behavior, they usually have difficulty providing loving support to their loved one.

If they do not side with their child wholeheartedly, even when he or she is wrong, they may find themselves emotionally blackmailed with the threat of not seeing their own child or the grandchildren. The end result is that they may suppress and deny their own feelings to hold on to what they have left.

Very rarely does the leaving spouse recognize the conflicting emotions his or her extended family is experiencing. That would create even more guilt, and guilt is the one thing the ex-spouse wants to avoid at this time. The avoidance of guilt leads to rationalization and excuses. It is often manifested by insisting that the extended family members have nothing to do with the former spouse. Many times the extended family members are helpless to say or do anything except stand by sadly and watch the disintegration of part of their world.

For a period of time, it may be necessary for the extended family to remain silent. However, it is a right and a loving act to hold people accountable for their actions. It is important for extended family members to acknowledge their own sadness and confusion and to affirm that they still care for their former son-in law or daughter-in-law and the children.

It is important for all family members on both sides to speak kindly to the children about both parents. That does not mean taking inappropriate behavior lightly or pretending it is not happening. There are times, depending on the circumstances and the ages of the children, when it may be necessary to verbalize to the children what they know about the situation. For example, if a parent is an alcoholic or abuser, it is important to tell the children that it is possible and all right to love their parent but to not like their behavior. That is an important lesson for all of us. It does no good and costs your own credibility to deny the obvious.

FRIENDS

Most friends just don't know what to do—causing them to be very uncomfortable. Do they try to counsel? Do they try to support both individuals? Do they tell one what the other is doing? Do they carry messages between the two? If they have a party, do they invite both of them? Do they tell both of them the other is invited? Do they include one or the other when everyone else in the group is part of a couple?

They may be thinking, "What if she goes after my husband now that she has none of her own?" Will she be asking my husband to help her with things around her house?" "What if my husband starts getting ideas when he sees his friend living a seemingly fun bachelor life again?" What if he starts hanging out at our house conveniently at dinner time?" "What if he decides my wife is easy to talk to, so he bends her ear all the time?"

Friends usually mean well, but in their discomfort they often back away from the friendship. Many divorced people feel abandoned by their married friends. It is bad enough they have been told by a mate that they are no longer lovable or desirable, but to also be forgotten by friends is deeply painful. Friends may just forget to include the divorced person. It is not that they mean to be unkind, but they only think in terms of couples when they plan social events.

If the divorcing couple's social life revolved around one of the spouse's work colleagues or clients or around a church community or club, it is almost impossible for both to remain involved as before.

Many divorced people become very sensitive about including their single friends if they themselves are remarried. Having experienced being left out themselves, they realize that it is not a significant problem if the number of places at the table are uneven! Interestingly, both males and females report they are more comfortable with an extra man or two at a gathering than with an extra woman.

Many friends try to be impartial and supportive. However, friendship does not mean ignoring the behavior of someone who is abusing the spouse or family. Friends, too, can live in denial about the realities of the situation, hoping things could work out. It takes courage, but real friends do not condone continued abuse by their silence or their actions. Silence can be deadly to victims.

The loss of friends is often unexpected and bewildering to those who are divorcing. It really hurts, whatever the reason. Mutual friends do not always know how to love and support both individuals without supporting bad or irresponsible behavior. Most friends can respond appropriately if, for example, a man leaves his family, provides no financial support, and wants the friends to join him on a cruise with his new girlfriend. However, most situations are not that obvious, and friends often find themselves choosing to deny reality to remain neutral. Unfortunately, many people find themselves in a compromised position of tolerating behaviors they loathe or cannot respect because they don't know how to say no.

It is a rare situation and a rare friend who can successfully balance both relationships very long. They have to be very careful and very honest with themselves and with the two individuals about loving and supporting both of them without contributing to or cooperating with either one in hurting the other.

Letting Go

What does it mean to "let go?" How does it feel?
What are the things that you want to "let go" of?
How about

- guilt
- trying to fix things
- anger
- chaos
- being a victim
- sadness
- perfection
- shame
- self-doubt
- worry
- the past
- fear
- confusion
- old beliefs
- powerlessness
- the need to control
- resistance
- being naive
- unhealthy relationships

Chapter 4

Add others that come to your mind. Now, go back and list an example of as many of these as you can. Then, describe what your life would be like if you could let go of each one of these.

What would you do instead?

How would your life be different?

What stands in the way of your letting go of each one of these?

The primary reasons we do not allow ourselves to let go of a person or of marriage are

- an unconscious hope that if we refuse to make a new life, we can keep alive what was and the hope that it might be again.
- the fear of making a new life with all the accompanying necessary adjustments.

"Letting go" is an important step in moving toward the stage of acceptance in the grieving process. Until it is done, full recovery and healing cannot take place. Even the decision to let go is only a beginning. The grieving process does not occur in a straight line; even as we are moving forward in the process, we move back and forth between the various stages. As we grow more comfortable with our decision to let go, we will find our trips back through the other stages of grief grow fewer in number and with more time between visits. We are then acting our way into new feelings instead of feeling our way into new actions.

Emotionally, letting go represents losing part of your old identity and history. Your marriage and your ex-spouse are part of who you were and they strongly influenced your picture of yourself and your place in the world. To let go of these things is like losing part of yourself. We naturally resist this loss. It is not easy to cut that cord permanently.

Letting go does not mean that you must completely forget about your marriage and former spouse. Comments such as "I've got to pretend it never happened" or "I won't ever mention my divorce to anyone so that I can ignore the whole situation" are more a reflection of the denial stage of grief than the acceptance stage. Your ability to move on depends on dealing honestly with the situation and working through it, not setting it aside. To ignore the situation is repression, not "letting go."

To let go in a healthy way does not mean you have to totally change everything, walk away from the responsibilities you have, or become a different personality. The task of letting go involves sorting through your life to find the good things, being thankful for them, and holding on to them. It also involves identifying what no longer works or serves any real purpose and replacing those things with something better.

Start with small things. Be willing to take one day at a time, beginning with baby steps. Eventually you will be able to move forward in life again with confidence.

Use these open ended statements to help you begin to take those steps toward letting go.

- I choose to let go of old, useless ways of thinking and will do the following things to replace them....
- One positive effort I will make this week is....
- This week I will initiate some social activity by....
- This week I will fill the void of being alone by....
- One positive thing I will do for my spiritual health this week is....
- I will strengthen my relationships with friends by....
- One thing I will do for God this week is....
- One thing I will do to help someone else this week is....

There are parts of the past you can never be free from. If there are children, the former marriage partners will be forever tied to each other in various ways through the children, even after they are grown. Your task in letting go is to not give the past a disproportionate power over your current and future life. One can learn to detach from unhealthy parts of the past while remaining healthily involved in the present situation, even if it includes people or situations related to your past.

To detach is not to stop caring about someone or some situation. It is to stand a good distance away, to stop trying to control the person or the outcome of the situation, and to allow the person to make his or her own choices. Detachment allows a situation to unfold with natural consequences. Detaching with love recognizes that there are things you cannot control. As you detach from a situation, you turn the control over to God.

ISSUES RELATING TO CHILDREN

As time goes by, it is sometimes possible to begin to see the traits in children that are disturbingly reminiscent of the problematic relationship that existed in the marriage. Alcoholism may become a problem for the child of an alcoholic. Unhealthy angry explosions or abusive behaviors by children may become new reminders of the situation you struggled to get away from. A daughter may become promiscuous even though her mother's similar behaviors may have led to the divorce.

These types of behaviors in children are often an indication the children were not allowed or did not know how to work through their grief issues, both at the time of their parents' divorce or in the years that followed.

Sometimes, imitating the behaviors of a parent is an unconscious attempt by the child to identify with or to feel close to the parent they are emulating. It is most often the parent of the same gender. While growing up, a boy learns what it means to be a man by the example set by his father—good or bad. The same with a daughter and her mother.

If children do not have the opportunity to process the experiences of divorce in a healthy way, there are many holes left in their understanding of what they should be and how they should act. Those holes will be filled with other role models that may not be positive.

It is not uncommon for children to turn on the "good" parent as a way of justifying their choices of following the other parent's lead. The children know better, but they have an unfilled need for the other parent that defies reason or logic. No matter what a parent does, a child has a need and love for him or her. Sometimes, emulating that parent is the only way they can express that need.

Children can stay lost in that mode for a long time. It is an especially deep pain to relive the same scenario of bad behaviors with a child that have already been lived with a spouse. It is a deeper wound. You cannot and do not want to divorce a child. During the time a child is acting out inappropriate behaviors, it may be necessary to find different, more effective ways of interacting with the child. Such a child may need extra time and space, much like in the story of the prodigal son (Luke 15:11-24). As you will recall, the father did not prevent the child going his own way (but I'll bet he counseled and warned him of dangers), nor did he go after him. But he waited (and I'll bet he prayed a lot), and he joyfully ran to meet his son when the son came to his senses and returned. This story could just as easily apply to a distraught mother with a restless, unsettled child. It doesn't have to be about money; it can be just walking away from what is right or what is healthy. Waiting and praying are tedious tasks of patience and faith.

Letting go is a lifelong process. All people have things that they must let go of apart from divorce. The letting go skills you learn while going through a divorce can be effectively used in other areas of life. Letting go does not mean giving up. The development of an active prayer life will assist you in the process of letting go (as well as all in other aspects of life). Through prayer you can name your concerns before God and then turn them over to God. In prayer you can experience God's grace and love that offer freedom from your past and strength to move on.

To live in yesterday is a waste of time—even God cannot change the past. It is not today that binds life, but it is the regrets of the past or fears of the future. We only have today. How today is lived determines the quality of tomorrow.

Chapter Four – Letting Go

Forgiveness

Forgiveness is a difficult concept to understand and harder still to practice. It has been used inappropriately and ineffectively. It is one of the most difficult things you will ever do, and yet, it is the most freeing. There is an instinctive resistance to it, especially when you are hurting or when you do not fully understand what it means. A wall goes up, your backbone stiffens, your countenance changes, and you can almost see bristles appear. The reaction is very real and very understandable, but the task of forgiveness is very important.

As Christians we recognize that none of us is perfect and that all of us stand in need of forgiveness. God's forgiveness is not something we earn but something that is given to us as a gift. This does not mean that God's grace is an invitation to do anything we want regardless of the harm it does to others. Forgiveness does not make us unaccountable for our actions. There are consequences to our actions. However, God's gift of forgiveness can free us from the bondage of our past actions and empower us to live lives that reflect God's love.

Just as God has forgiven you, you hold the power to forgive others. Forgiveness is not dependent upon the actions of another person. Likewise you also have the power to accept forgiveness. You cannot make another person forgive you, and you cannot force another to accept your forgiveness.

Forgiveness is an important step in freeing you from past pains and injuries. It does not necessarily lead to the reconciliation of the marriage. Forgiveness does not mean that you resume an unhealthy relationship. It does involve giving up the need to extract payment or invoke punishment. In forgiveness you take back the power you have given to the other person to hurt you or to control your actions. It frees you to be able to carry on without the burden of bitterness. The healing and freeing power of forgiveness for yourself is not dependent upon the other person accepting the forgiveness. Although accepting the forgiveness may be important for the other person's healing and recovery, it is not necessary for your own healing.

The decision to forgive and the act of forgiveness will bring about introspection. It is helpful to examine the things that you have done that have caused pain or harm to another (including your former spouse). Honest reflection upon your own life and experiences can help you face hidden guilt that may be slowing your recovery process. It can also assist you in identifying behaviors that you do not want to repeat.

Remember that in both giving and receiving forgiveness, God is with you. You can come to the Lord with your skepticism, your anger, your fears, and your sadness. As the Scriptures say "neither death, nor life, nor angels, nor rulers, nor things present, nor things to come, nor powers, nor height, nor depth, nor anything in all creation, will be able to separate us from the love of God in Christ Jesus our Lord." (Romans 8:38-39)

Love is an important motivation as well as a vital ingredient in forgiveness. One motivation is love for yourself, a desire to be healthy and free of the burden of hate and resentment.

Forgiveness is a command by God. So is love. (See Luke 6:32-38). Both are actions of obedience. You may think that if you do not feel love for that person, there is no use in trying to forgive. But God's commandment to love does not insist that we have to like or even approve of another. Jesus loved those who called to have him crucified. As Christians we are called to love all God's people, even those whose actions are harmful. Love is a very misunderstood word—cheapened by overuse and misuse. Unconditional love is not unconditional approval of one's behavior. Mature love includes caring and truth.

So, forgiveness is complicated and, at the same time, simple. It is never easy. In the context of divorce, it is hardly ever a joint venture. The healing power of forgiveness can help you to find joy and fulfillment in your current life. It can also have a healing effect on others, particularly children affected by the divorce.

In summary, forgiveness is a conscious choice to act. Forgiveness is a loving act that does not ignore truth. Forgiveness is a holy command and is part of God's character. Forgiveness opens our eyes to a deeper level of understanding of ourselves and others. Without forgiveness, we hurt ourselves and those innocent people around us. Not forgiving does not punish the guilty, it gives them control of our lives. Not forgiving blocks our own growth and well-being.

To rush to forgiveness too soon—before the grieving process is finished—often results in a false forgiveness. Forgiving ourselves is the hardest part. Most of the time we do not recognize that we are angry at ourselves or that we hold ourselves responsible for

- not being good enough
- not being smart enough to have avoided or prevented the divorce
- not knowing the right things to do or say to fix the relationship
- feeling frightened at the prospect of starting a new life
- not being able to "save" the marriage
- the embarrassment, guilt, and shame

Realizing how much God loves us, how willing and anxious God is to forgive us, to restore us, and to enfold us in loving arms makes it easier for us to see our need and to forgive ourselves. We cannot forgive others unless we can also forgive ourselves. Forgiving ourselves opens the door for forgiving those who wronged us.

SECTION TWO

Then Grow

Accepting Responsibility

The word *responsibility* means having the ability to respond. What separates the ability to respond from an automatic reaction is the interjection of thought and a decision. In the absence of this, you still act, but it is more likely to have negative consequences.

Without making a thoughtful decision, one remains reactionary. That leads to impulsiveness, without regard to the consequences. As humans, God has given us the ability to analyze, to evaluate, to discern, and then to make well-considered, responsible choices.

The test of responsibility is accountability. We are accountable for our choices. Whether it is to a spouse, to a boss, to those we lead, to society, to our friends and extended family, to our neighbors, or to our communities, we are measured by how well we honor our responsibilities. And, of course, even if we could escape all of the above,

Chapter 6

we are still accountable to God. God knows our deepest yearnings and our greatest fears. We cannot fool God.

We are responsible for our own integrity and for building or rebuilding our own character. Although God is with us, God has also given us the gift of free will, the ability to choose for ourselves whether or not we will act with integrity.

For most people, divorce is a crucible in which they discover their own levels of maturity and responsibility. It is also an occasion to see those levels of your ex-spouse. There may be surprises, disappointments, or validations of what you already knew. There may be some of all three.

CHOICES

You choose whether or not you will be responsible, and you are responsible for the choices you make. The greater the level of maturity, the greater the willingness to be responsible. The greater the willingness to be responsible, the more likely one is to make good, solid decisions about life.

Each step of the recovery process presents new choices that have to be made. Some of the choices you make will not be as good as others. There is a difference between making an error in judgment while trying to do the right thing and a conscious choice to do the wrong thing. Even poor decisions, however, can create opportunities for learning and growth.

Looking at people who have experienced divorce, it is clear that many have gone on to happier, more peaceful lives—the result of making positive choices or of having learned from their negative choices.

For those going through divorce, there are the obvious choices that must be made concerning lifestyle changes. Now it is not just yourself as it once was before your marriage, but perhaps you with children, an accumulation of possessions, and more obligations, all making demands of your time and resources.

You must make choices. That is how you negotiate the demands. To try to avoid making choices is impossible and may cause you to become immobilized. It is important to remember that you do, indeed, have options, maybe more than you initially think you have.

Sometimes, the most important choice you make is the attitude you bring to the situation.

Some of the most difficult new choices you have to make relate to dating, friendships, and sexual involvement. Many studies have shown that it is not helpful to jump into a romantic relationship (whether that be dating or remarriage) immediately after your divorce. At a time when you may be feeling lonely and insecure and feel a deep need to be touched, held, appreciated, valued, and cherished, you may not find this a welcome message. The need is greater than ever, but so are the dangers. Some counselors recommend at least two years after the final divorce decree before getting seriously involved with someone new. For some people, even that is not enough time. One of my observations is that the longer persons remain single, the more selective they become and the happier they become with themselves.

Society places great pressures on "being with someone." There are unspoken, and often tactless spoken, messages about being single, alone, unattached, an unclaimed blessing. Interestingly, for a single man, the insinuation is often that he is selective, a prize eluding capture. But for a woman, it is often that she has not yet been able to catch anyone. Attractive women frequently get comments such as, "If you aren't married, there's no hope for any of us."

Statistically, however, it is impossible for all singles to find someone. Not remarrying is not the end of the world. Remember Jesus himself was a single person. As delightful and euphoric as being in love can be, it is not the most important thing in life. One's integrity in meeting responsibilities and caring for one's children is more important and has a longer lasting impact on you and everyone around you. Your wants must take second place to your needs and your children's needs.

Until you are content with who you are as a single person, you are unprepared to remarry. The emotional work to be done after a divorce is essential. Grieving, adjustment, charting a new course—all are work, but the rewards are priceless. The amount of work these tasks represent to each of us may vary, but no one is ready to remarry without having dealt with them.

Once you have worked through your own recovery process, you may still not recognize whether or not a potential marriage partner has worked through his or her own recovery. It is not enough to be beyond the sadness and settled into a new lifestyle. You need to have learned from the past so you are able to recognize and avoid old familiar patterns that may be harmful.

Time and again, we hear of someone who repeats old behaviors in a new relationship. We are all at risk of another poor relationship if we do not learn from our previous experience. It takes time to learn to recognize your own danger signals. Once you are "in love" or "in lust," you can explain away all sorts of things in favor of the pent-up needs and desires.

Chapter Six – Accepting Responsibility

It is not unusual for a person to have a crazy period of time where he or she throws caution and values to the wind in response to the pain and disillusion of divorce. While it may be common and understandable, that does not mean it is a healthy or productive way to deal with the divorce. The consequences of irresponsible behavior can be destructive and even deadly.

Another common occurrence is to have a transitional relationship—one that seems very appealing at the time, one in which you get too deeply involved too soon, one that can be recalled later with some embarrassment. You may not recognize it as a transitional relationship, but it is usually the first big romance after a divorce. The need to be wanted, to be validated as a lovable man or woman, or to be connected can make someone seem very attractive. You discover later that you rushed into the relationship too quickly, and it is not what you hoped it would be.

In trying to allow yourself the time you need before reconnecting, it is helpful to find productive and fun ways to fill time and to use energy. Finding a circle of other single friends to talk to, to do things with, to create opportunities for having fun and learning to laugh again can be very productive.

What does the church say about sexuality for the newly single? The *Book of Discipline of The United Methodist Church* makes the following statement, "We recognize that sexuality is God's good gift to all persons. We believe persons may be fully human only when that gift is acknowledged and affirmed by themselves, the church, and society. We call all persons to the disciplined, responsible fulfillment of themselves, others, and society in the stewardship of this gift.... Although all persons are sexual beings whether or not they are married, sexual relations are only clearly affirmed in the marriage bond. Sex may become exploitative within as well as outside marriage. We reject all sexual expressions that damage or destroy the humanity God has given us as a birthright, and we affirm only that sexual expression which enhances that same humanity. We believe that sexual relations where one or both partners are exploitative, abusive, or promiscuous are beyond the parameters of acceptable Christian behavior and are ultimately destructive to individuals, families, and the social order." (¶ 65)

This entire book is about responsibility and choice. No one is immune from the effects of irresponsibility. In these days, with the vast numbers of people infected with one of the many sexually transmitted diseases, there is a practical, physical, life-and-death reason to behave responsibly. If not, you can hurt yourself, and you can be an instrument of pain to someone else.

Another common mistake among some is to continue having sex with your ex-spouse. It complicates issues and slows the recovery process. If there is any hope of reconciliation for the marriage, it lies in resolving other underlying issues, not in continuing a sexual relationship.

Sex is one of God's best gifts. It is one of the most missed parts of marriage for someone who is divorced. But no one ever died for lack of having sex, and sex was never intended as a recreational sport. The Bible teaches that sex is not an end unto itself. It is intended for pleasure (and fun) within an intimate, covenant relationship. Marriage is a covenant between a man, a woman, and God. Yet Jesus never married. It is okay not to be married.

Much of what we humans see as need is really want. Sex is one of those things. If we place an undue amount of emphasis on the act of intercourse, we can find ourselves being controlled by that desire or controlling someone with that promise. The way in which we act responsibly in our sexual attitudes and behaviors says much about our maturity, our integrity, our sense of self-worth, and our concern for others.

Instead of just "letting things happen," take a proactive position with your life. Choose friends, behaviors, and activities that will affirm you in all areas. Talk to the Lord about your needs and wants. God cares about you and all of your concerns—even sexual ones. Prayer is a powerful tool. Commit your needs to God's keeping and ask God to guide your choices.

THE CHOICE TO MARRY AGAIN

Blending families is not easy. It is difficult to anticipate and adequately prepare for the myriad of issues that present themselves. Each person added to the family multiplies the number of relationships that have to be dealt with. For example, if a man and woman who each have a child get married, you have the following relationships: husband and wife, mother and child, stepmother and child, father and child, stepfather and child, stepsibling and stepsibling. That is a lot of relationships to bring together at one time and to coordinate successfully. And that does not include the additional dynamics of the noncustodial parent relationship with the parent, stepparent, and each child—or each of the members of their respective extended families.

Remarriage further subdivides parents' time, energy, attention, and focus with the child, who is already divided by the divorce between the two biological parents and their extended families. What may appear to be a help to a difficult situation and a return to normalcy, can actually compound the difficulties in the situation. This is not to say that remarriage with children is impossible, but it is important to be aware of the issues that will need to be resolved.

In our discomfort with all the changes we are forced to confront in a divorce and with our intense desire to regain some sense of normalcy, it is easy to view remarriage as the definitive answer to all problems. If you are considering marrying again as a way to "solve your problems," you are very likely to be disappointed.

Having said all this, if after a healthy time of grieving and growing, you find yourself in a committed and loving relationship and you want to remarry, consider all the issues, get some professional advice to help you deal with the issues you are facing, and proceed with caution, caring, and patience. Premarital counseling is very valuable to those who are considering remarriage and marriage.

CHANGES

Life is all about change—constant change. We establish routines and traditions to cushion and stabilize life in the midst of change. Change is part of growing. Without it, things become stagnant and die. As long as we live, we are adjusting to change. Some changes we enjoy, some we endure. Some changes we choose, other changes are a result of the choices others have made.

Make a list of the negative changes you have experienced. These might include things like moving, financial adjustments, changes in friends and jobs, and so forth.

_____

_____

_____

_____

_____

Now make a list of the positive changes you have experienced. These might include things like participating in new activities, spending more time with family, making new friends, and so forth.

_____

_____

_____

_____

_____

Now look over your lists again. Are some of the negative changes really opportunities for positive changes? What do you need to do to turn the negative changes into positive opportunities?

How will you begin to build a new life, one that you choose, develop, and define? Change can be opportunity. Once you see that, it diminishes your sense of loss, your feelings of victimization, and it triggers your ability to let go of the past and move forward in the recovery process. A sure sign of recovery is when people cease to be self-absorbed and self-protective and begin to reach out to others.

CHALLENGES

Of the many challenges one is forced to face in divorce, the biggest one may be finding the courage and strength to look challenges squarely in the eye and believe that you can meet them. Some challenges will be met better than others, some more quickly than others, and some more easily than others. There will be new challenges set before you continually.

If you are the custodial parent of children there is the ongoing challenge of meeting escalating financial obligations, working, keeping house, spending quality time with each child, and finding even a small amount of time for yourself. There is the added pressure of assuming all the children's parenting needs on a daily basis. The work and responsibilities remain the same, but there is half the time and "people power" to accomplish them.

One of the most helpful ways to meet these challenges is to learn to explore options as quickly and as well as possible. Each option will have its own consequences. You always have a minimum of four options about any action you are considering.

Chapter Six – Accepting Responsibility

1. You can do it and like it.
2. You can do it and not like it.
3. You can not do it and like it.
4. You can not do it and not like it.

It is important to learn to see more than the one option. Then you will begin to believe that there are more possibilities for greater quality of life than you can see at the moment. Identifying options is especially helpful during the grieving and adjustment period.

Some wonderful books have been written on the art of negotiation, exploring options, finding a bigger view of the world and ourselves in it. Some of these are listed among the resources at the end of this book.

The things discussed so far provide an overview of the current challenges and the potential new challenges. By laying the foundation for a new beginning, you can begin to rebuild. The basement floor is the grieving process and the working through what has already happened to you. The basement walls are the beginning supports for the main part of the house—your new life. How you build those supports and the materials you use will greatly affect the strength, the size, and even the beauty of the rest of the house.

This is your one and only life. It is not a dress rehearsal. Choose to be proactive, not reactive.

Balance

One of the laws of nature is the need for and the gravitation toward balance. The intervention of a significant emotional event, such as divorce, automatically throws one's life off balance. The grieving process (especially the final stage of acceptance) facilitates the return to normalcy or balance.

Picture a table with four legs—each leg representing one of these things:

1. Work (what we do to give ourselves a sense of accomplishment.)
2. Family and Friends (relationships that give our life meaning and purpose.)
3. Values (the guiding beliefs and principles, including religious ones, around which we order our lives.)
4. Recreation (what we do to renew and refresh ourselves.)

If one of those legs is slightly shorter than the others, what will happen if you place something on top of the table? Depending on the size, weight, and position on the table, it may or may not roll off.

A life in which one of the four areas is short can still maintain a sense of balance. All of us at one time or another have one of the legs slightly shorter than the others. In a healthy life, the shorter leg will, at some point, rebalance itself with the others. Meanwhile, the other three legs can stabilize the table.

What happens if one leg is dramatically longer than the others? Everything placed on it will fall to the floor. This is an example of what happens when our life is in crisis. It is impossible to rebalance without a major adjustment.

A balanced life does not necessarily mean that there is an equal amount of time devoted to each aspect of your life. For instance, work usually takes eight to ten hours of a day. Sleep, which is part of the re-creating, renewing process, takes about eight hours. That leaves six to eight hours of the day to be divided between family and friends and other things that we value.

There are times when one of these areas may demand an extra portion of our day. An overtime project at work, illness of a family member, or vacation time may temporarily take up more of your time at the expense of the other things in your life. When concentration on any one area goes on too long, it can throw us out of balance.

SPENDING TIME
WISELY AND CREATIVELY

One of the tasks of recovery of any kind is healthy self-examination. We need to look at the overall picture of our lives to see how well we are balanced. This is an ongoing process that becomes more important with readjustment to a significant loss, such as a divorce. It is important to monitor your life and to take the necessary steps to correct imbalances.

The following exercise will help to evaluate how you are now spending your time. The circle represents a whole day. How are you dividing it up? Use pie wedges to indicate how much time you are spending on various activities. Use the second circle to show changes you would like to make to create a more balanced life. What area surprised you? What area needs the most work to balance your life better.

Chapter Seven — Balance

Make a list of fifteen things you really enjoy doing. Circle the items that you are currently doing less frequently than you would like. Note the date of when you last did each thing you listed. Write down the amount of money it costs to do each thing. Think about how much fun and laughter is currently in your life. Plan to do at least one thing this week that will be fun. It is important to make an investment in yourself. Self-care is not selfish. It is a requirement for a well-balanced life.

Things I like to do	Date	Cost
1.		
2.		
3.		
4.		
5.		
6.		
7.		
8.		
9.		
10.		
11.		
12.		
13.		
14.		
15.		

KNOWING YOURSELF

How do you describe yourself? Are you more of a spender or a saver, a leader or a follower, impulsive or decisive? Do you prefer solitude or having lots of people around? What are the character traits that have influenced the way you relate to others? Are there changes you would like to make regarding the way you approach situations and relationships?

In the list below circle the words that apply to you. Add additional words that describe your positive characteristics.

academic	accepting	active
adaptable	adventurous	adaptable
affectionate	aggressive	alert
ambitious	artistic	assertive

attractive	calm	capable
careful	charming	cheerful
clear-thinking	clever	competent
competitive	confident	conscientious
considerate	cooperative	courageous
creative	curious	daring
decisive	dependable	determined
dignified	discreet	eager
easy-going	efficient	emotional
energetic	enterprising	enthusiastic
fair	farsighted	firm
flexible	friendly	generous
gentle	good-natured	healthy
helpful	honest	humorous
idealistic	imaginative	independent
informal	formal	conservative
liberal	traditional	ingenious
intelligent	kind	likable
logical	loyal	mature
methodical	meticulous	modest
natural	obliging	open-minded
optimistic	organized	original
outgoing	patient	persevering
pleasant	poised	practical
prudent	purposeful	rational
realistic	reasonable	reflective
reliable	resourceful	responsible
robust	romantic	self-confident
self-controlled	sensible	sensitive
serious	sharp-witted	sincere
sociable	spontaneous	stable
steady	strong	strong-minded
sympathetic	tactful	teachable
thorough	thoughtful	tolerant
tough	traditional	trusting
trustworthy	understanding	verbal
versatile	warm	well-mannered
wholesome	wise	witty

You are the only person you will live with your entire life. Parents, friends, spouses can leave or die, your children grow up to lives of their own, but you remain. It is vitally important to your health and well-being that you like the person you are. Be someone you would like to spend time with.

I once read that if you say you are bored, it is because you are boring. There is so much to see and do, so much to learn, so many ways to make life exciting. Invest time and energy in yourself. You are worth it! Do not just be a human being, be a human "becoming." You are a valued child of God.

Then What?

Unfinished Business

A major reason for mental and physical illness is unfinished business, unresolved issues that get in the way of our recovery. Unfinished business may include issues related to denial, grief, forgiveness, or unmet responsibilities.

Twelve-step recovery programs for a wide variety of addictions are found throughout the country. Regardless of the issue being faced, the steps to the program assist participants in dealing with unfinished business. The goal is to really know yourself, to face things that need to be faced, and to make amends for harm that has been done.

As you examine your own unfinished business, you may find the steps of the twelve-step programs helpful. They include

1. Admitting that you have a problem that is making your life unmanageable.
2. Believing that there is a power greater than yourself that can restore you. (For Christians that power lies in the saving, healing, and redemptive power of God.)
3. Making a decision to turn your life over to God.

Chapter 8

4. Making a searching and fearless inventory of your life.
5. Admitting to God, to yourself, and to another human being the exact nature of your wrongs.
6. Recognizing that you are ready to have God remove all these defects of character.
7. Humbly asking God to remove your shortcomings.
8. Making a list of all persons you have harmed and being willing to make amends to them all.
9. Making direct amends to such people wherever possible, except when to do so would injure them or others.
10. Continuing to take personal inventory and when you are wrong promptly admitting it.
11. Seeking through prayer and meditation to improve your contact with God, praying for knowledge of God's will and the power to carry that out.
12. Practicing these principles in all areas of your life.

Each life has its own story. Each of us has our own demons to face and our own messes to clean up. Sometimes, if you have really hurt someone and you go try to make amends, it may be necessary to stand still and let them vent at you and tell you how you hurt them. Take it. This is especially true with your children. It is important to say, "I'm sorry I let you down." Being able to express their own feelings of pain and betrayal can be an important step in their own healing.

Making amends means swallowing false pride and setting aside defenses. It means taking responsibility for yourself and your own behaviors. It means being willing to have relationships restored—whether with ourselves, others, God, or all three.

If a Christian who has gone through recovery was responsible for the decision to divorce, that person may be able to use this information and experience to work toward restoration of the marriage. That person now has new insights and new tools. In some cases if neither partner has remarried, reconciliation may be an option to explore.

The completion of your own recovery is the work you do on yourself. It does not matter what your former spouse does or does not do. That is none of your business. It does not matter how he or she receives your efforts to finish your own individual business. That, too, is none of your business. It is what you do about finishing your own business that matters.

The Future

You have walked through the different phases in recovery. You have gained some insight into the dynamics of loss and grief. With time, the road before you will level out and you will see things more clearly, with new eyes.

The next step, after working through your grief, is to accept the new identity you now have. You are a single man or woman. Maybe you are also a single parent. You are a valued child of God who has much to teach and offer others.

You can learn to take care of your car. You can do some home repairs or arrange for them to be done. You can buy a car or a condo. You can learn to cook, decorate your own place, carpool, or whatever is necessary. You can survive and even thrive. You can learn to go places on your own and really enjoy yourself. You will surprise yourself and everyone around you at what you can do.

Be creative. Try new things. Make new friends. Do not accept someone else's stereotype of being divorced. They do not know if they have

Chapter 9

not been where you are. You know. You know what you need to do, or at least how to find out what you need to know.

Remember that no one has your fingerprints but you. You are unique and unrepeatable. You are God's very own creation. God loves you and wants the very best for you—as you want the best for your child or someone you dearly love. God knew you and loved you before you were born. As the Psalmist proclaimed

Where can I go from your spirit?
    Or where can I flee from your presence?
If I ascend to heaven, you are there;
    if I make my bed in Sheol [hell], you are there.
If I take the wings of the morning
    and settle at the farthest limits of the sea,
even there your hand shall lead me,
    and your right hand shall hold me fast. (Psalm 139:7-10)

Wow! What reassurance! What a promise! How important you are to God!

It is okay to fail too. That is part of the learning process. Whenever you risk, there are bound to be some mistakes or failures. But think of the possibilities!

Set some goals—both short-term and long-range. Begin by writing down all of the hopes and dreams you have. Give your imagination a free rein. Then look at each item you have listed. What steps would you need to take to make that hope a reality? What you have always thought was a pipe dream may, in fact, be possible with a little planning and hard work.

One thing that many newly single people do not do is plan for the future. In the midst of trying to make it from one day to the next, they often forget about planning for retirement or thinking about what they want to be doing five or ten years from now. When single people start making plans for their own future, it is another sign they are recovering.

Short-term goals are usually goals that you hope to accomplish in an identifiable period of time. The may include things that you plan to do today, this week, this month, or even in the next year. Short-term goals may include usual, mundane things. Sometimes just getting out of bed or doing daily chores is a worthy short-term goal. Other short-term goals could be things like getting a job, finding opportunities to network with others, or joining a health club.

Short-term goals help move you toward long-term goals. For example, the short-term goal of finding a job may move you toward the long-term goal of financial independence. Joining a health club may be a step in a long-term goal of becoming more physically fit. The hopes and dreams you listed earlier may become your long-term goals. The steps you need to take to make those goals a reality become your short-term goals.

Write down your goals and select target dates by which you plan to accomplish each one. Keep a record and check off goals as you accomplish them. It helps to keep you on task and on target. It gives you a feeling of pride and accomplishment. A word of warning: Do not let this plan become so rigid that you miss other opportunities and joys in life or that you berate yourself if you miss a target date.

Make sure some of your goals include personal needs or desires. Perhaps you need better nutrition, more rest, some recreation, or time just to clean out your closet and drawers. Take good care of your health. Someone is depending on you, and it is not just children or loved ones. It's **YOU**!

Chapter Nine – The Future

Singles Groups

Do any of these questions sound familiar? How do people meet each other? What are the new expectations regarding behavior? Is it acceptable for women to call men for a date? Are men still supposed to pay the bill and open the doors all the time? If he buys me dinner, will he expect sex at the end of the evening? If I don't make a pass at her, will she think I don't like her or that there is something wrong with me? What about kissing on the first date? What about anything else on the first date?

It may have been a long time since you have dated or have been around people other than couples in a social setting. Moving into social events on your own may be uncomfortable. The world has changed since you were single before. You may wonder about what is now considered appropriate behavior.

Newly divorced men and women can easily be swept up in an unhealthy popular image just because they are unsure of themselves and others.

Chapter 10

As you adjust to life as a single person again, you may find it very helpful to find a group of other singles where, together, you can find understanding and support.

There is the need to just be with people, to find people to do things with, to find space and time to regain equilibrium. Some people arrogantly avoid singles groups, thinking, "I don't want to hang around with a bunch of losers. My situation is different. I'm not a loser." Of course you're not. But neither are they.

It is that same arrogance that can keep us lost because we refuse to look at a map or ask for directions. It takes a measure of humility to admit you have a need. That humility is the gateway to getting your need filled.

A church singles group has the marvelous potential for creating opportunities to meet people's needs. Participation in a singles group can help restore confidence in yourself and in the future. It can provide a warm, comforting, place where healing can happen. It can expand and broaden your view of life and the world. It may be a way of pushing you into contact with people you would never think of getting to know, people who can challenge you into new, exciting directions easily missed. It can be a real turning point and a way to facilitate recovery. It provides a good measure of your own healing to begin to reach out to help others.

Church singles groups may offer social events, service projects, worship experiences, intentional opportunities for spiritual growth such as Bible studies and covenant groups, and programs for personal growth. Many singles groups sponsor divorce recovery support groups. (That may be why you are currently reading this book.) For many, singles groups provide an entry point for participation in the total life of the church. Each singles group takes on the complexion of the members. However as a church group it has the responsibility to reflect God within the organization and operation of the group. I like a comment from one who is very actively involved in a singles group I know. She said, "We are not out to create a strong Christian singles ministry, but we are out to create strong Christian singles who can minister to others."

A word of caution is needed as you enter a singles group or as you help your church to establish one. Not all who attend a singles group are coming because they want to find a supportive caring atmosphere where they can grow with other Christian singles. Because many people who participate in singles groups are just emerging from a painful situation, it is likely that any singles group will have members who are still in a fairly fragile personal state. Knowing this, people with harmful and selfish motives may seek out singles groups as place to find others they can exploit. Just because you meet someone at a church occasion does not mean that you can automatically assume that person has the same values and goals as you.

Just like any group within the church, singles groups need clear guidelines and policies that create an atmosphere of Christian community where members are safe. Each group needs

1. a competent counseling or referral system for singles who need help.
2. a process for dealing with conflict within the group.
3. clear standards and reporting procedures that deal with inappropriate and dangerous behavior.

Many churches are currently developing churchwide policies to help prevent abuse and harassment within the church and to deal with it in a way that protects the victim if it does occur. If your church does not have policies in place, you may want to encourage their development.

What Now?

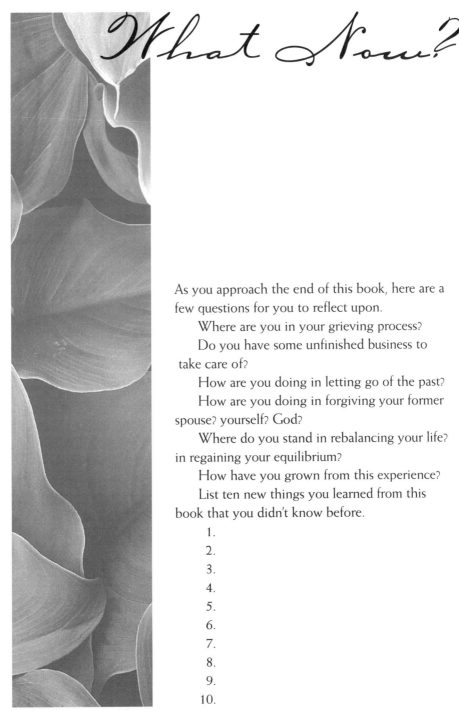

As you approach the end of this book, here are a few questions for you to reflect upon.

Where are you in your grieving process?

Do you have some unfinished business to take care of?

How are you doing in letting go of the past?

How are you doing in forgiving your former spouse? yourself? God?

Where do you stand in rebalancing your life? in regaining your equilibrium?

How have you grown from this experience?

List ten new things you learned from this book that you didn't know before.

1.

2.

3.

4.

5.

6.

7.

8.

9.

10.

Chapter 11

Put a check by the ones that are applicable to your life or that you want to use in making positive changes. List ways you can incorporate those changes into your life and the results you expect.

_____

_____

_____

_____

_____

Draw a picture in your mind of the "new you." Describe yourself. How do you look? How do you carry yourself? What is your attitude like? What are you doing with your time and your life?

_____

_____

_____

_____

_____

_____

_____

_____

_____

_____

_____

_____

_____

_____

HOPE FOR THE JOURNEY

It takes courage and strength to set a new direction for your life. But you are not alone in the journey. Here are some words of hope and promise to guide you along your path.

> God is our refuge and strength,
> a very present help in trouble.
> > (Psalm 46:1)

> Do not fear, for I am with you,
> do not be afraid, for I am your God;
> I will strengthen you, I will help you,
> I will uphold you with my victorious right hand.
> > (Isaiah 41:10)

> Be strong and bold; have no fear or dread of them, because it is the LORD your God who goes with you; he will not fail you or forsake you.
> > (Deuteronomy 31:6)

> For surely I know the plans I have for you, says the LORD, plans for your welfare and not for harm, to give you a future with hope. Then when you call upon me and come and pray to me, I will hear you. When you search for me, you will find me; if you seek me with all your heart.
> > (Jeremiah 29:11-13)

> So we can say with confidence,
> "The Lord is my helper;
> I will not be afraid.
> What can anyone do to me?"
> > (Hebrews 13:6)

> Do not worry about anything, but in everything by prayer and supplication with thanksgiving let your requests be made known to God. And the peace of God, which surpasses all understanding, will guard your hearts and your minds in Christ Jesus.
> > (Philippians 4:6-7)

Chapter Eleven — What Now?

A Guide for Group Leaders

Starting Again is designed to be used as part of a church-related divorce recovery program. Eight session plans are provided to help guide a group facilitator in leading the program.

GROUP SIZE

Each group should have at least four participants and no more than fifteen. If you have more people who want to participate, consider holding two sessions at different times or recruiting additional facilitators and dividing into two or more groups.

TIME

Each session is designed for about an hour and a half. The times listed by each activity are approximate guides.

MATERIALS NEEDED

Nametags
Chalkboard and chalk
Newsprint and felt-tipped markers
Paper
A copy of *Starting Again* for each participant

FACILITATOR QUALIFICATIONS

Facilitators of divorce recovery groups should be skilled in group dynamics and in active listening. Potential leaders include pastors, social workers, counselors, and others who have had training and experience in facilitating small groups. While facilitators do not need to be divorced, they should have a working knowledge of the issues divorced people face. It is often helpful to have two facilitators, one male and one female. Divorced facilitators should be suffi-ciently through their own recovery process so that they will not impose their own agenda on the group. All facilitators must be individuals of high moral character who have the emotional maturity to deal with people who may be very vulnerable. This program is not designed to provide psychological therapy for participants. Facilitators need to be able to recognize issues that are beyond the group's ability to deal with; in those cases they must make the appropriate referrals. Facilitators need to be alert to the possibility that some group members may have ulterior motives for participating in this type of program and take appropriate steps to make sure that no one in the group is victimized.

GROUND RULES

It is important for each group to develop ground rules for how the group will conduct itself. These ground rules should include issues related to confidentiality, attendance, participation, socializing outside of the group, and so forth. Facilitators may need to remind members of the ground rules and to help members hold one another accountable for abiding by them. While it is common for strong friendships to develop during the course of the program, it is best if group members agree not to begin a dating relationship with anyone in the group during the duration of the program. Facilitators should never enter a romantic relationship with a member of the group during the course of the program or immediately afterward.

AFTER THE PROGRAM

Some groups may decide to continue to meet occasionally after the program ends. Sometimes someone may request to repeat the program with a new group. This should be discouraged. Each group has its own personality and someone who has been through the program will bring expectations of what the group "should" be like based on the previous experience. This is likely to negatively affect the group dynamics. People who wish to repeat the program should be guided into another type of group that will be more appropriate for their current situation.

CHILDCARE

Providing on-site childcare will allow some people to participate who would not otherwise be able to do so. Churches may want to offer a divorce recovery program for children that meets at the same time as the *Starting Again* group.

Session 1

GOALS

To help participants
- recognize losses that have occurred because of their divorce.
- develop strategies for expressing the feelings caused by the losses.

SESSION PLAN

1. Introduction (10 minutes)

Arrange the chairs in a circle and invite participants to find a place as they arrive. Introduce yourself by telling your name and one thing about yourself. Ask the person next to you to do the same thing and then to repeat your name and the item you mentioned about yourself. Continue around the circle with each person adding his or her name and something he or she wants the group to know and then repeating the information given by those preceding. Conclude the icebreaker by naming yourself, all the participants, and their information. Welcome the participants, and describe briefly the purpose of the program.

2. Establish a Group Covenant (15 minutes)

Explain that since this program will be a group experience, it is important to have agreed-upon ground rules. Help the group come to agreement on important issues and write those agreements into a covenant. A sample covenant might look like this:

- We will start promptly at (time) and conclude at (time).
- Participants will commit to attending every session. If an emergency arises and someone cannot attend a session, he or she will contact the group facilitator before the session.
- Everyone will be treated with respect.
- We will listen carefully to each other and not interrupt.
- Participants (including the facilitator) will not begin a dating relationship with one another during the length of the program.
- We will respect each other's personal space and will obtain permission from each other before we offer any physical demonstrations of support,

such as hugging.

- Information shared within the group shall remain confidential.
- Since we recognize that each person is responsible for working through his or her own recovery, we will support each other but will not try to "fix" one another.
- We will pray daily for each person in our group (including the facilitator).
- We will hold one another accountable to abide by this covenant.

Write the covenant on a piece of newsprint and post it in a place where it can be seen. Save the covenant to be posted at future sessions. (You may want to give each person a typed copy of the covenant to sign.)

3. List and Discuss Losses (20 minutes)

Ask the participants to think about the losses they have experienced. As people call out items, record them on the chalkboard or newsprint. Through your body language and comments, show appreciation for the contributions. Allow for some discussion. Do not force anyone to contribute. (It is common to have 20 to 30 losses listed.)

Help the participants identify similarities and differences in the things mentioned. For example, are some losses more often experienced by men and others by women? Are some things mentioned more often than others? Are there any items that sparked a new awareness for someone? Are there other things that need to be added to the list?

4. List and Discuss Feelings (20 minutes)

Follow the procedure described in step 3 to list and process the feelings identified by the group. Help the group connect particular feelings to particular losses. Remind the participants that feelings are not good or bad and that we can choose how we respond to our feelings. Help the group distinguish between thoughts and feelings. Save the lists of losses and feelings for referral in future sessions.

5. Break (10 minutes)

Consider having light refreshments and beverages available. You may want to develop a sign-up list for people to volunteer to bring refreshments.

6. Expressing Feelings Constructively (20 minutes)

Divide the participants into smaller groups of four to five. Assign each group several of the feelings that were identified in the previous exercise and ask them to list as many ways that they can think of to constructively express those feelings. (As participants do this exercise you may find that some people begin to tell their stories related to the feelings. An important part of this program involves giving people an opportunity to tell their stories. Throughout the sessions create a variety of opportunities for this to happen.)

After the small groups have had an opportunity to develop their lists, ask them to report back to the larger group. (Some of the responses may be humorous. Humor is often an effective tool in dealing with uncomfortable subjects. Laughter helps build community.)

If no one mentions keeping a journal, suggest that this is another helpful method for expressing feelings. Encourage the participants to identify one thing that they will try to do this week to help express their feelings.

7. **Review and Close** (10 minutes)

Help the participants to review by asking them to answer the following questions:

• What was most helpful to you in this session?
• What could be improved?
• What new insight did you gain that you can use in your life?

Suggest that during the week participants read the first chapter of *Starting Again*.

Close with a prayer such as:

Dear God, we thank you for giving us feelings. We also give thanks that you are with us in the midst of all of our feelings: joy and sadness, happiness and grief. Guide us in our steps toward recovery. Thank you for the assurance that you love us and are with us. In Christ's name we pray. Amen.

(A personal note or phone call during the week will help participants feel welcomed and appreciated)

Session 2

GOALS

To help participants

- understand the grief process and how it relates to divorce recovery.
- identify where they currently are in the grief process.

SESSION PLAN

1. Introduction (10 minutes)

Welcome any new members. (No new members should be allowed to join the group after this session.) Reread the group covenant. Then ask each person to think of a loss they experienced at the age of eleven or twelve. Give the group a few moments to reflect individually and then ask them to respond with the following statement:

A loss I had when I was eleven or twelve was _____. I remember feeling _____.

2. Review (15 minutes)

Invite participants to recall things that they remember from the previous session. Record the responses on newsprint or on a chalkboard.

3. Examine the Grief Process (30 minutes)

Have the participants review Chapter 2 in *Starting Again*. Then lead the group through a review of each of the stages of grief. As you review each stage, use some of the following questions to help stimulate discussion and reflection:

- How have you experienced this step?
- What was helpful to you in this step?
- What would you want to tell someone else who is going through this stage?
- Where do you think you currently are in your grieving process?
- Have you ever observed someone who "got stuck" in a stage and was unable to move on?

4. Break (10 minutes)

5. Relate the Stages of Grief to Personal Feelings (20 minutes)

Have each participant locate the list of feelings they identified last week

(p. 14). Ask them to go through the list and try to assign a stage of grief to each feeling. They may assign more than one stage to any particular feeling. There are no right or wrong answers to this activity. The purpose is to help participants see where they have been, to identify where they are currently, and to gain some clues about what the next stages may hold for them.

Allow time for discussion so that participants can report any insights they have had.

6. Review and Close (10 minutes)

Help the participants to review by asking them to answer the following questions:

- What was most significant part of this session for you?
- Is there anything we could do differently that would be helpful?
- What new insight did you gain that you can use in your life?

Suggest that during the week participants read the second and third chapters of *Starting Again*.

Close with a prayer such as:

Gracious God, we know that grieving is a part of life and that even Jesus wept in sorrow. We give thanks for the healing that comes through the grieving process. Bless each person in this group and help us all as we move through our grief to know that you are with us. Grant us courage to face the feelings that come with grief. In Jesus' name. Amen.

Note: There is not a session designed around Chapter 3, "Special Issues." The issues that are mentioned in this chapter will probably come up in discussions throughout the program. Use the information in this chapter to help guide discussions as the issues emerge.

Session 3

GOALS

To help participants

- become aware of things that may be impeding or slowing their recovery process.
- learn how to begin to let go and to continue to move forward.

SESSION PLAN

1. Introduction (10 minutes)

As the participants gather, give everyone slips of paper and ask them to write down three things they are working on letting go of. These could include things like: getting revenge on your ex-spouse, the need to be a victim, the need to tell your story over and over again, trying to turn the children or others against your former spouse, efforts to control your former spouse, and so forth. Explain that the things they are writing down will not be shared with the rest of the group unless someone wants to. When they have finished, ask them to fold the papers and keep them to use later in the session.

2. Review (15 minutes)

Ask the participants to recall things they remember from the previous week. Invite them to comment on any insights they have had during the week related to discussions the group has had so far.

3. Discuss "Letting Go" (30 minutes)

Have the participants read Chapter 4 of *Starting Again*. Lead a discussion around the issues that are discussed in the chapter. You may want to use an example from your own experience of something you knew you needed to let go of and yet held on to. Identify for the group what kept you from letting go.

Help the participants make a list of things that divorced people may need to let go of. Record the things that are mentioned on newsprint. For each item mentioned examine the reasons someone may have for not letting go. Reasons could include things such as denial, the need for sympathy, and self-pity. Then examine the fears that are associated with letting go of the things listed.

Discuss ways of following through on decisions to let go.

Session Three – A Guide for Group Leaders

4. Break (10 minutes)

5. Symbolize "Letting Go" (15 minutes)

Provide an opportunity for participants to symbolically "let go" of those things that are holding them back in their recovery process. Three suggested methods are:

  a) Build a fire outside or in a fireplace and let the participants burn the slips of paper they wrote on at the beginning of the session.

  b) Make a ceremony of tossing the slips of paper into a trash can.

  c) Place the pieces of paper inside balloons. Fill the balloons with helium, and offer a prayer as participants release the balloons. (Because of environmental considerations, releasing the balloons outside is not recommended.)

Whatever method you choose, reassure the participants that they only need participate if they are ready.

6. Close With Prayer (10 minutes)

For many people the previous activity is a very powerful, emotional exercise. Give anyone who wants to the opportunity to express any feelings they have about the experience. Then close with a prayer something like:

Dear God, We know that we all have things that we need to let go of. We ask for your guidance and blessing as we give up those things that are keeping us from lives of joy and freedom. We know that you love us, and we place our lives in your constant and everlasting care. Thank you Lord. Amen.

Session 4

GOALS
To help participants
- understand the importance of forgiveness.
- learn how to forgive themselves and others.

SESSION PLAN
1. Introduction (10 minutes)
When everyone has arrived, ask each group member to complete this sentence:

If I could talk to God face-to-face about my divorce, I would ask God
_____, and I would tell God _____.

2. Review (15 minutes)
Ask the participants to recall things they remember from the previous week. Invite them to comment on any insights they have had or changes they have made during the week related to their recovery process. Some people may want to report on the progress they have made in letting go.

3. Discuss Forgiveness (30 minutes)
Begin this discussion by reminding the group that not everyone is at the same point in their recovery process. While some in the group may not be at the stage of forgiveness yet, the information presented in this session will be helpful when they reach that point. Ask everyone to read Chapter 5 of *Starting Again*.

On a sheet of newsprint or on a chalkboard write: Forgiveness is not.... Ask the group to develop a list of things that complete the phrase. Possible examples include: forgiveness is not allowing bad behavior to continue; forgiveness is not excusing inappropriate behavior; forgiveness is not having unhealthy boundaries; forgiveness is not going back into an abusive relationship.

Then, on another sheet of newsprint or on a chalkboard write: Forgiveness is.... Ask the group to again think of things that complete this phrase. Possible examples include: forgiveness is giving up the need to "get back at"; forgiveness is claiming the power to take charge of my life; forgiveness is ceasing to control my ex-spouse; forgiveness is believing that I am a beloved child of God.

Use the responses to both phrases as a springboard to further discussion about forgiveness.

Explain that one way to begin to identify who we need to forgive is to examine areas in which we are experiencing anger. Ask the participants to think back to the session on the grief process and remember the stage of anger. Have the participants silently identify those they need to forgive. Remind them not to forget themselves.

Let those who want to share their thoughts do so now. Recognize that for many people this evokes strong feelings. Part of the healing process is the opportunity to express feelings in a safe and supportive environment.

4. Break (10 minutes)

5. Accepting God's Forgiveness (15 minutes)

Give each person a blank sheet of paper. Make sure there is enough privacy so that no one can see what anyone else is writing. Explain that this exercise will be done individually and that the group will not be discussing what people write down. Ask them to make a list of all the sins they have committed.

When everyone has finished, have them draw a line across the bottom of the list. Then tell them to write these words below the line: Paid in full. Love, Jesus

6. Closing (10 minutes)

For many people this will have been a very emotional session. Do not push people to speak, but allow an opportunity for anyone who needs to share feelings or thoughts to do so.

Write the following prayer on the chalkboard or newsprint. Ask the group to say the prayer together, each silently praying the names to fill in the blank.

Lord Jesus, I thank you that you have forgiven my sins. Grant me the love and strength to forgive those who have hurt me, whose names I now place before you, _____. Help me to remember that since you have forgiven me, I can also forgive myself. In Jesus' name we pray. Amen.

Session 5

GOALS

To help participants
- begin to make responsible decisions about their future.
- begin to consider future healthy relationships.

1. Introduction (10 minutes)

When everyone has arrived, ask each group member to complete these sentences:

If money were not a issue, the first thing I would do is _____. If I could change jobs, I would really like to _____. My ideal date would be _____.

This is a thought-provoking exercise and should be done without much discussion about the responses. Remember the power of humor, and do not be surprised if some of the responses generate some lighthearted moments.

2. Review (15 minutes)

Point out that this session begins the second half of the program. Ask each participant to reflect on what has been most significant for them in the past four sessions. Invite people to share their thoughts, and record their responses on newsprint or a chalkboard.

Review the goals of the first four sessions. Let the group discuss whether or not these goals have been met. If some of the goals have not been met, discuss what the group could do to help meet them.

3. Discuss Opportunities for Growth (30 minutes)

Ask everyone to read Chapter 6 of *Starting Again*. Give everyone time to list the positive and negative changes they have experienced on pages 68-69. After everyone has had a chance to work on their own, invite the participants to name the choices, changes, and challenges they are facing. Common responses include things such as risk-taking, trust, fear, commitment, dating, and remarriage. Record the responses on newsprint and use the items listed as a focus for further discussion.

4. Break (10 minutes)

5. Think About Future Relationships (15 minutes)

Ask each person to write down what they would look for in a dating relationship or in a spouse. Then have them reflect on how that list differs from what they would have written before their marriage and divorce.

Divide into small groups of three to five people. If possible include both men and women in each group. Have the groups discuss the things they listed.

6. Review and Close (10 minutes)

Ask the group to answer these questions:

a) What new insights have you gained about yourself from this session?

b) What changes, if any, do you anticipate in your future relationships with the opposite sex?

c) What new information, if any, did you receive from this session?

Close by reading Psalm 32:8:

"I will instruct you and teach you the way you should go;

I will counsel you with my eye upon you."

Pray a prayer something like:

Dear God, thank you for your promises to guide us as we face new choices, changes, and challenges. Grant us wisdom to make responsible choices, flexibility and creativity to deal with the changes, and courage to face our challenges. In Christ's name. Amen.

Session 6

GOALS

To help participants
- begin the task of self-examination.
- examine ways to create balance in their lives.

SESSION PLAN

1. Introduction (10 minutes)

After everyone has arrived, ask each person to write one activity that he or she really enjoys. Then have them write how much it costs and how long it has been since they have done the activity. If it has been some time since they last did the activity, ask them to reflect upon why it has been so long. If they have done the activity recently, have them think about how they felt afterwards. Invite participants to tell the rest of the group what they have written.

2. Review (15 minutes)

Invite the participants to make observations about anything that has been discussed in previous sessions. This is also an appropriate time to talk about what they are learning and how it is affecting their lives.

3. Discuss Balance in Life (30 minutes)

Have the participants read Chapter 7 of *Starting Again*. Review the four elements of a balanced life. Have the participants do the exercises presented in the chapter. After each exercise encourage the group to discuss insights and observations related to the exercise.

4. Break (10 minutes)

5. Plan for the Future (15 minutes)

Divide into smaller discussion groups of three to five. Let each group discuss the challenges and choices they are facing related to creating a more balanced life. Encourage the group to discuss possible strategies for implementing the changes they want to make.

6. Review and Close (10 minutes)

Reassemble the group, and let each small group give a brief summary of the choices and challenges the group discussed and the implementation strategies.

Close with a prayer something like:

Dear God, we thank you for the balance of the created world and the gift of freedom to make choices. Help us to make wise choices that lead to fulfilling work, loving relationships, strong values, and constant joy and renewal. Help us to lead lives that honor you. In Jesus' name. Amen.

Session 7

GOALS

To help participants
- free themselves of the past.
- set short-term and long-term goals.
- explore options for social opportunities.

SESSION PLAN

1. Introduction (10 minutes)

After everyone has arrived ask each person to name someone he or she admires and explain why. Then ask participants to describe themselves as they would like to be.

2. Review (15 minutes)

Ask the participants to recall important learnings from the previous session. Invite group members to share any significant steps in their recovery process that have occurred since the last session.

3. Discuss Unfinished Business and the Future (30 minutes)

Ask the participants to read Chapters 8, 9, and 10 of *Starting Again*. Review the stages of the twelve-step recovery programs. Remind the group that these are helpful guides even if a person is not dealing with an addiction. Encourage the participants to think about their own unfinished business and how these steps might be helpful in resolving those issues.

Have each person make two lists, one of short-term goals and the other of long-term goals. Invite participants to tell their goals to the rest of the group.

Discuss the social opportunities participants are currently enjoying and develop a list of other options that could be explored. Include a discussion of singles groups. If your church has a singles ministry, you may want to share information about the program. If there are no singles groups in your community the group may want to consider beginning one after they have completed this divorce recovery program.

4. Break (10 minutes)

Session Seven — A Guide for Group Life

5. Examine Personal Unfinished Business (15 minutes)

Ask the participants to make their own private list of the unfinished business they need to attend to—amends that need to be made, relationships that need to be repaired, and so forth. Challenge the group members to develop a concrete plan for dealing with their unfinished business. (For many people this may be a very emotional activity.)

6. Review and Close (10 minutes)

Sometimes it is easier to carry through a difficult task if we make a public commitment to do so. If there are group members who want to talk with the group about the plans they made in the previous activity, allow them to do so. As in all activities, do not force anyone to share.

The next session is the final session of this program. If the group wants to conclude with a party or potluck, make plans and discuss any special arrangements.

Invite the participants to comment on the most significant part of the session. Close with a prayer something like:

Gracious God, thank you for the lessons of the past and the promises of the future. We know that you want the best for us and that you have a wonderful plan for each of our lives. Help us to be led by your Spirit in our journey into tomorrow. In Christ's name. Amen.

Session 8

GOALS

To help participants
- review what they have learned from the sessions.
- celebrate the completion of these sessions.

SESSION PLAN

1. Introduction (10 minutes)

After everyone has arrived ask the participants to introduce the person on their right by saying the person's name, some things they have learned about the person, and something about the person that they appreciate.

2. Review (20 minutes)

Ask the participants to read Chapter 11 of *Starting Again*. Allow time for each person to privately answer the questions posed in this chapter and complete the list of things they have learned.

Ask the participants to name the things they have learned during the sessions. Record responses on newsprint or on a chalkboard. Then ask the group to reflect on the most helpful parts of the program. Ask for suggestions on how the program could be improved for future groups. Encourage the participants to complete the *Starting Again* evaluation on page 112 and mail it to the address listed on the evaluation.

3. Appreciation Exercise (30 minutes)

Give each participant a poster-sized sheet of paper and a felt-tipped marker. Each person will need a different color. Have each person write his or her name in large letters at the top of the paper, and tape the paper to the wall. (If the setting does not allow for taping things to the wall, place the papers on tables.)

Ask the participants to circulate among the papers and write one or more positive adjectives on each person's poster. The adjectives should describe the person whose name is at the top of the poster. (Examples include caring, fun lovable, interesting, and so forth.)

After everyone has written on each sheet, have the participants retrieve sheets. Let the group members tell the rest of the group how their sheet m

Session Eight – A Guide for Group L

them feel, what surprises them, and what they particularly like. Close this activity with a prayer that affirms the gifts and abilities of the group members.

4. Celebrate

Conclude the session with a party, pot-luck dinner, or another fun activity to celebrate the end of the sessions. Some groups will want to maintain contact with one another and will want to distribute a list of names, addresses, and phone numbers. The group may want to consider planning a get-together a few weeks or months from now to check with one another. Some group members may be very satisfied with the divorce recovery program but not be interested in maintaining further contact with the group. Each group has its own personality and its own experience with this program.

Suggested Resources

Caring Enough to Confront: How to Understand and Express Your Deepest Feelings Toward Others, by David Augsburger (Scottsdale, PA: Herald Press, 1980).

Development Through Life: A Psychosocial Approach, by Barbara M. Newman (Pacific Grove, CA: Brooks Cole Publishing Company, 1998).

Growing Through Divorce, by Jim Smoke (Eugene, OR: Harvest House Publishers, 1995).

Letting Go: A 12-Week Personal Action Program to Overcome a Broken Heart, by Zev Wanderer and Tracy Cabot (New York: Dell Publishing Company, 1987).

Reconcilable Differences: Healing for Troubled Marriages, by Jim Talley (Nashville: Thomas Nelson, 1991).

Second Chances: Men, Women, and Children a Decade After Divorce, by Judith S. Wallerstein (New York: Houghton Mifflin Company, 1996).

Single to Single, edited by Douglas L. Fagerstrom (Wheaton, IL: Victor Books, 1991).

Surviving the Breakup: How Children and Parents Cope With Divorce, by Judith S. Wallerstein and Joan B. Kelly (New York: HarperCollins Publishers, Inc., 1996).

What Children Need to Know When Parents Get Divorced, by William L. Coleman (Minneapolis: Bethany House Publishers, 1998).

Women Who Love Too Much: When You Keep Wishing and Hoping He'll Change, by Robin Norwood (New York: Pocket Books, 1986).

You Gotta Keep Dancin': In the Midst of Life's Hurts, You Can Choose Joy, by Tim Han (Colorado Springs: Chariot Victor Publishing, 1998).

Evaluation

Please take a few moments to help us evaluate this resource.

Rank these statements

1= Strongly agree

2= Agree

3= Disagree

4= Strongly disagree

____ The resource helped me in my own recovery process.

____ The book provided helpful information.

____ I would recommend this resource to others who are divorced.

____ The session plans were easy to follow.

Tell us a little about your self.

Church _____ City _____ State _____

Which of the following apply to you?

____ Facilitator of a *Starting Again* group

____ Participant in a *Starting Again* group

____ Read *Starting Again* without participating in a group

Additional Comments

_____
_____
_____

Please send this evaluation to:

quisitions Editor, Family and Life Span Ministries

ral Board of Discipleship • P.O. Box 840 • Nashville, TN 37202

uld like to receive information about other Discipleship Resources products, please fill

rmation below.